The Complete Handbook For

COMMUNITY THEATRE

From Picking the Plays

To Taking the Bows

The Complete Handbook For COMMUNITY THEATRE

From Picking the Plays To Taking the Bows

by Jean Dalrymple

DRAKE PUBLISHERS INC.
NEW YORK • LONDON

Published in 1977 by
Drake Publishers, Inc.
801 Second Avenue
New York, N.Y. 10017

Design: Harold Franklin

Library of Congress Cataloging in Publication Data

Dalrymple, Jean.
The complete handbook for community theatre.

Bibliography: p.
1. Amateur theatricals. 2. Theater – Little theater movement. I. Title.
PN3151.D29 792'0222 77-6925
ISBN 0-8473-1579-7 - pbk.
ISBN 0-8473-1624-6 - cloth

Printed in the United States of America

CONTENTS

An amateur is "one who cultivates an art without pursuing it for a living." Community Theatre begins for amateurs with intense discussions about the play. Here the play being studied is *The Effect of Gamma Rays on Man-in-the-Moon Marigolds. (Picture courtesy of Long Island Studio Theatre of Lindenhurst, N.Y.)*

Preface

THE COMMUNITY THEATRE, the theatre of the devoted amateur, and the professional theatre, whose members work with equal devotion to make a living from it, have more in common than they seem to realize. They strive with equal diligence for that illusive rainbow, the smash hit, yet it happens on Broadway as seldom as it does in Community Theatre. We have all seen some extraordinarily fine productions put on by amateurs. (I use the word "amateur" throughout this book in its first meaning, as set forth in the dictionary: *"Amateur . . . from amare . . . to love; one who cultivates an art without pursuing it for a living."*) We also have seen some extraordinarily inept failures on Broadway, sometimes with half a dozen "big names" involved. And after every resounding failure on Broadway the question arises: "How could that producer, that director, those stars—all those people who are so experienced in show business get into such a mish-mash to begin with?" There really is no answer because there are so many answers.

There was one famous case, some years ago, where a well-known playwright telephoned a popular "bankable" star, who was a friend of his, and asked, "How would you like to co-star in my new play with Jane Doe?", naming another star who was even better known. "I'd love to!" was the answer, whereupon the playwright called Jane Doe and asked if she'd like to co-star with Joe Bloke. Same answer, "I'd love to!" With no hesitation the playwright then called a successful Broadway producer who believed in "names" and asked, "How would you like to produce my new play co-starring Jane Doe and Joe Bloke?" You know the answer. "I'd love to!" The play was put in rehearsal and as work went on each person involved found himself thinking, "I really don't see what Jane Doe liked about this script . . . but then Joe Bloke liked it . . ." and so on and so on. It was disaster time right through to the opening night, with all concerned either ashamed or afraid to say they'd made a mistake. So they all grimly waited for the critics to say it for them.

That, of course, is a very exceptional case. I am pretty sure it couldn't happen today, when each production costs upward from a quarter of a million (one set, two characters!) to a million and a half dollars. The producer who believed in names would today at least read the script, which that particular man later on admitted that he never had. But even so, he said, he probably would have produced it anyway, because both Jane and Joe liked it!

I tell that story because something like that can happen and has happened in Community Theatre, too; not that the script was never read, but just that two favorites in a company wanted to do a friend's play and no one else involved with the company ever had the courage to say right at the beginning—perhaps lacking the conviction through insufficient knowledge or experience—that it would be a flop.

In the general run of theatre work it is my personal conviction that success or failure depends on the skill, the "know-how," or the lack of it, on the part of the people involved from the very beginning of the project: they who in the first place select the play, the director, the scene designer, the stage manager, the press agent—everyone who must give 95 percent of his talent and endeavor (5 percent off for coffee breaks and gossip) to bring all the pieces together and reach that crucial and often magic moment when the house lights go down and the stage lights come up for opening night.

So, for those gallant amateurs in virtually every town, city and village in this vast United States who make Community Theatre flourish, this little handbook of suggestions, hints, and factual information is written in an attempt to lighten the burden of the people involved—many of whom I know and greatly admire—and to help them in their decision-making. It is also an attempt to answer some of the myriad questions that seem to arise in any theatre undertaking, no matter where or when, time and time and time again.

I have the temerity to do this because I have been part of the theatre all my life, and for lo these many years I have tried to seek out the elusive ways and means of working through the difficult to achieve the beautiful.

—Jean Dalrymple
New York, 1977

chapter 1

Getting Started

BEING THE HEAD of a community or "little" theatre and being its chief administrator does not have the glamour for some theatre buffs that acting on its stage or directing its plays has, but if that is your part in the project it can be a soul satisfying avocation when you do it well and the theatre succeeds. Of course, I am taking it for granted that you and perhaps a few of your friends have felt a need for an amateur theatre in your community or neighborhood and that you are now going ahead with your plans for handling the myriad details that lead up to a successful opening night.

I am also assuming that you have found the physical place to present your plays. Perhaps you have sold the Board of Education on the idea of using the auditorium of the local high school. Perhaps a church group has offered you their facilities. I have seen little theatres flourishing in any number of unexpected places—a supermarket basement, a store front, an apartment that had been gutted and rebuilt with stage and dressing-rooms, a deserted fire-house. In the country there are always the barns, some in apple pie order and others in a state of semi-disintegration, but all worth considering.

Depending on the nature of your community, quarters for your acting group may be secured by an active campaign to tie it in with some sponsoring organization. Religious and scholastic institutions, as just noted, are among those most commonly offering such arrangements. Fraternal and club organizations, Chambers of Commerce and other business oriented organizations, may prove amenable to providing quarters and perhaps even some further degree of sponsorship. The facilities of a town hall, an American Legion headquarters, a Rotary, or Kiwanis, or Elks meeting place have provided many a drama group with a stage, or at least an in-the-round playing area to mount its productions.

There are, incidentally, many advantages to pursuing sponsorship beyond the mere providing of theatrical premises. A theatre group which exists as part of a larger organization—be it church or club, community or business—will find real advantages in being able to draw upon the resources of that organization. Publicity can be facilitated since the larger group will probably already be geared for it. The membership of the larger organization, eager to help "their drama group," will provide both a potential audience and a potential source of ticket sales to their families, friends and neighbors. They will have a rooting interest in the success of the acting group and this interest can be turned into the sort of cooperation which facilitates the borrowing of props and costumes from shopkeepers, the lending of tools for the building of sets, or perhaps help and advice in the building itself, the design and sewing of costumes, and all of the other many activities which will grow out of the needs of each individual production. Still, all of this will come later. The initial—and most important—advantage, will be the securing of the space to put on plays.

Once you have your "theatre," it is important to choose a name for your company, if you have not already done so. That name must become widely known as soon as possible. The news of your infant endeavor must be spread widely, both by word-of-mouth and by published announcements in your local or neighborhood publications, as well as by radio, if that is possible. Have no hesitation in asking for help from the news media, for the formation of a theatre group is news in every sense of the word and it is not difficult to get complete cooperation. A new theatre company, whether professional or amateur, is an event that will have far reaching consequences for all concerned as well as for the area.

No publicity approach should be overlooked. Besides the more obvious media—radio, TV, major newspapers—you should not neglect the small, more restricted outlets. These can include church newsletters, PTA bulletins, Chamber of Commerce and American Legion and fraternal and sororal communications. In some larger cities there are neighborhood, or housing project weekly newspapers and newsletters which should be sent announcements. In smaller communities flyers can be distributed door-to-door, and handbills and posters can be put up on the town bulletin board, or in the window of some prominent store.

Most important, a list of outlets for publicity should be made up at the time your group is formed. This list should be constantly added to and monitored so that it is up to date. As your first project progresses, it should be routinely publicized with follow-up announcements. The sequence of announcements might be as follows:

1) *This is to announce the formation of a drama group to be called (name of group). The drama group will be sponsored by (name of sponsoring organization). Its performances will be given at the (name of auditorium). Membership in this group is open to all. The tentative date for a meeting to select the first play to be performed will be (date and time).*
2) *The (name) Drama Group has decided to present (name of play), a drama by (author). The tentative date set for the first performance is (date). A casting call—open to all who are interested—will be announced.*
3) *(Name) has been selected to direct (play), the first production of the (name) Drama Group sponsored by (name of sponsor) and scheduled to go on the boards at the (name of auditorium) on (date). (Name of director)'s previous credits include directing (list plays) plus acting in (list plays) with the (name of acting group or groups). (Note: If the director has no previous credits, make much of his or her debut and the real-life background being brought to the particular play.) (Director's name) would like to announce an open casting call (date and time) to all who are interested. No previous acting experience necessary.*
4) *(Name), director of the (name) Drama Group's production of (play and author), would like to announce that (actress' name) and (actor's name) have been selected to play the leads in the drama. (Actress' name) has previously appeared in (list credits). (Actor's name), a prominent barber of this city, is making his debut in the challenging role of (character's name). Other members of the cast include (list names and previous experience).*
5) *The (name) Drama Group announces that its production of (play and author) directed by (name) and starring (principals' names) will have its first performance at the (name of auditorium) on (date). Subsequent performances will be given on (list dates). Tickets are available from (whoever is in charge of ticket sales and whichever local store or stores will cooperate) and from all members of the (name) Drama Group.*

With each step in the production of the play—no matter how small and seemingly unimportant—still more announcements of this kind should go out to the publicity list you are shaping.

Now let us move on to the supporting cast of non-actors you must assemble if you wish to turn your fledgling group into a functioning company. To do this, you must let it be known that anyone interested in joining your group is welcome and that not only actors or folks who think they would like to act are invited, but all people interested in the many other duties that make play production possible: directors, designers, stage managers, publicity directors, sound men, make-up experts or not so expert, and so on. It is important, too, that everyone know that all these workers are equally important. In community theatre there is no "caste system" as there seems to be in the professional theatre. A good property man or electrician can be as vital to the success of the venture as the leading actor, and should be given the proper deference. Young people who apply and who do not qualify for any of these many functions can be pressed into service as ushers. Pleasant and efficient ushers, by the way, are an important part of good public relations, as are pleasant and efficient ticket sellers or box office people. If not ushers, then the young people might like to become "gophers," those who "go-for" whatever is needed on the run, usually coffee, it seems. No one who shows any interest at all should be turned away without your finding out his or her latent abilities. Often the people who come to you are extremely shy, but the very fact that they did come is a proof that they want to be helpful, and it is worth a bit of digging into their psyches to uncover just what it is they can do. Sometimes you discover surprising talents. Even if there are none, ask them to become members, if you are going to have a membership listing, and ask them to help your project by giving you the names and addresses of their friends who might like to join and buy tickets.

I am addressing this to the one or two people who are responsible for running the theatre, but I realize that there are many community theatres which are operated by a board of directors. In my experience, it seems that that is not always the most effective or most desirable method. As the saying goes, "A camel is a horse designed by a board of directors." The theatres which seem to achieve success virtually from the time of inception usually are those relying on the judgment and ability of one person, or two in tandem, often husband and wife. It is easy to see that much of the indecision and wasted time in roundtable discussions can be avoided if the one or two people in charge make the decisions and present them with logical reasons to a board or committee which can then vote on them with a minimum of deliberation, although you can be sure of one or two voices being raised before the result is tallied. Once you have selected a staff and enrolled enough neophytes who are willing to perform on your stage, it is time to select your first play. This is the most serious step you will take at this point. It will be discussed in detail in the next chapter. Here, however, are some general rules to keep in mind when selecting your first production.

Take no chances. Don't be arty, and certainly don't be *avant garde*! The average theatregoer doesn't want to be a patron of the arts unless he is also being amused or emotionally stirred, preferably the former. The first play, therefore, is just about the keystone of your future.

Because today's audiences—from the todler to the great-grandparent—have been watching the work of most of the world's most important actors, directors, writers and producers on television, they are apt to be very aware—albeit subconsciously—of what is good and what is poor on the stage of your theatre. Some people who have never seen "live" actors before—and there are too many of them—are disenchanted at first. Others are enthralled. But all are critical.

If a famous Broadway comedy hit has recently been made available for community theatres, by all means let that play be your first choice. Even if you are not too sure of the calibre of your actors, you can be sure they will make a pretty good stab at it, for it will be fresh and exciting for them as it unfolds. And your audience will come to it without preconceived notions of how it should be done, since probably none of them will have seen it. That also can assure you good attendance, a plus toward the firm establishment of your theatre.

If such a windfall is not on the horizon, then choose a play which is difficult to damage, something with strong situations and characters, either dramatic or comic, such as, for instance, *Plaza Suite*. In fact, *Plaza Suite* is a good choice for your first play. Actually, it is three one-act plays, and although usually played by the same actors throughout, it can be done by three sets of actors and three directors, making an important division of work for all. It also will give your audience the opportunity of seeing the work and talents of several of the new actors in good leading roles, in which they will bend their best efforts to make personal hits. The one set for all three acts or plays is also helpful and lessens difficulties in that department. (A more detailed discussion of the advantages of one-act plays as vehicles for amateur groups along with suggestions for other one-acters which might be performed will be found in the following chapter on play selection.)

When, say, *Plaza Suite* has been selected, you will next choose your three directors. If you have been fortunate, you will have three people who have come to you who are eager to direct. It is always wise to pick the people who very much want to do a job, and it is often disastrous to press the work on someone who is diffident about his ability to handle it. Nepotism is a deadly sin in amateur theatre. Reject it. You may have a strong desire to build up your wife or husband, son, daughter or lover as the permanent director for the plays of your company, but unless the talent and the desire to direct are there, forget it. There is a woman I know who is a force in a well-established community theatre I visit from time to time who always insists upon having her husband handle the sound, when sound is called for. The only difficulty is that he is pretty deaf! Still, he gets to do the sound because he "loves sound." The results are usually quite odd.

If you have decided to do three one act plays or *Plaza Suite*, and have appointed your three directors, deciding that that is not only the best, but the least difficult way to go, each of the directors will then hold auditions to make their selections for the casts. All the people you have corralled as actors will be notified, and this is a good time to make a general announcement that anyone else who would like to take part may audition. Perhaps you will add to your ranks this way.

While this is happening, as was outlined before, the person handling your publicity should be spreading the news of the latest developments and activities. Members of the drama group, or of the sponsoring group, or perhaps even just friends of members, may come in handy here as in other areas. An artist can hand-letter posters which may be distributed locally. A photographer can supply pictures for a display showing the play in rehearsal. A printer can make up leaflets.

It is at this relatively early point in the formation of the group that the person in charge should sit down and make a list of *human* resources available to the group. This means not just those people who may be helpful with publicity, but anybody and everybody who may be helpful in all areas and at different stages of the play's production. Ideally, such a list will include the following:

A carpenter (amateur or professional) to help with the building of backdrops and doorways with doors that open and close without pulling down the scenery around them.

A dressmaker or seamstress (amateur or professional) to sew costumes and draperies and to make emergency repairs.

An audio person who knows how to time and splice a tape for sound effects. (Such a person might also handle sound effects during the actual performance.)

An electrician who can do the necessary wiring to arrange your spotlights and dimmers where they are needed to achieve the desired effects.

A beautician to handle make-up.

Providers—which is to say a whole sub-list—the longer the better—of friendly storekeepers, manufacturers, wholesalers, etcetera, who may be called upon to lend furniture, and appliances and sundries for sets and props. (A cooperative antique dealer will prove to be a major asset to any drama group.)

A trucker to haul major items from lender to borrower and back.

The list given here is, of course, only a partial one. Your list will be dictated both by the needs of the play you intend to put on the boards and by the people available to you. One further word of advice about it though: Save it! Make it an ongoing list from the formation of your group and its very first production through every play that you present. Each of these plays will have special needs and when you solve them, you will have added to the human resource list available for your next production.

The same principle applies to your early publicity. The shopkeepers who are kind enough to display your posters once will probably cooperate in all your future endeavors. A pattern will have been established. They can be invited to a dress rehearsal. Consider that it may be a better idea to entice them into selling as many of your tickets as possible to their customers than to sell them a mere pair for themselves.

Sell as many tickets in advance as you possibly can. You should have a good mailing list by this time, and a letter can be sent to everyone on it, announcing the first play, with the date of its opening, time of performance, and the prices of the tickets. An order blank should be at the bottom of the letter which can be torn off and returned with a check. You could include in this letter a special invitation to join the cast and staff at the opening night party after the performance.

The opening night party, as will be discussed, should be a lavish affair which includes strategically invited guests. But no matter its importance in that sense, its main reason for being really has to do with the cast and all others who have actively worked on the play. It is their efforts being celebrated, their pressure valve being released, their champagne cork being popped.

An incident involving one drama group I know illustrates the role of the party. It happened on that rehearsal night which comes to all groups as opening night draws close when everything goes wrong. Somebody fluffed a line and a shouting match broke out between two members of the cast. Another cast member walked off the stage in disgust and tripped over some loose electrical wiring, yanking it loose from its moorings. This led to an argument concerning sockets between the lighting man and the sound effects man. And all this time the stage manager was chewing out a prop girl who was close to tears. The director sat back and watched her production going to pieces before her very eyes.

"How can you put up with all this?" a spectator asked her. "All this emotional turmoil! Doesn't it tear you apart? It's not as if you were professionals doing it for money! What could possibly make this much effort and emotional drain and physical work and frustration worthwhile?"

To which the director calmly replied: "The cast party!"

It's true. But one must experience it to understand it. Actors who have vowed never to speak to each other again once the play is over may be found at the cast party in each others arms. The sound effects person and the male lead will be guffawing loudly over the doorbell that never rang. The ingenue's lipstick—on her stage lover's face through the whole last act—will finally be wiped off with a handkerchief dipped in scotch, and cooed apologies will be given and accepted in the cameraderie of the occasion. And the director—maligned and whispered about and even cursed through all the weeks of rehearsal—will now be toasted for her pulling together of the impossible dream, the astuteness of her judgment, her intrinsice theatricality, and her wisdom in pushing them all out there for the second curtain call. (Amazingly enough, it will probably be at the party that the cast will present the director with some pertinent gift in gratitude for her cajoling and harassing and perhaps even bullying them into giving the performances for which they are all now so busy giving each other congratulations.)

The party usually takes place after opening night. But you should plan to give your first production not just that one performance, but several. It is frustrating after all the hard work involved in getting started, to have an exciting opening night, a hit show, and no opportunity to enjoy the results. Your actors will appreciate a chance to make up for any small boo-boos they may have made. This is very important for their egos and for their confidence in future work. Also, if the play has been a hit there can be a substantial "window sale" at the subsequent performances.

But everyone connected with the production should already have been urged to take upon himself the responsibility of selling tickets to the opening night. A definite number can be allotted, or promises can be extracted to sell, say, at least five pairs. As they sell they can entreat the buyers to in turn try to sell five more pairs. Well, at least two or three.

This sort of chain merchandising works very well, for even if the ticket buyers can sell only one pair they "spread the word" and help to make friends for your company. Beware of those who oversell, however. You don't want to end up antagonizing people! We used a form of chain reaction at the New York City Center to successfully build up "The Friends of City Center," our sustaining and supporting members. Each person already a "Friend" was sent an invitation entitling him and a guest to attend a dress rehearsal, the guest to be someone not already a "Friend." Then at intermission a good speaker—perhaps one of the actors—would come before the curtain and ask those people present who were not already "Friends" to please join and to in turn try to bring in at least one new "Friend" before the season's end. This approach can be used in your theatre to increase your subscriber membership or to sell tickets to your forthcoming attraction.

If, after your scheduled rehearsals, you feel the play is not ready, that the actors are not secure in their lines, for instance, or there is no rhythm to the performance, postpone the opening. No matter how much opposition you meet, postpone it! Your first public showing must be as perfect as you can make it. Anything less could be disastrous. So no matter how many people are disappointed because they have made special plans for your announced opening night, just soothe them with honeyed words and a new definite opening date, perhaps a week later. You will be forgiven when they see a first-rate performance; they will never forgive you if you stick to your original date and give them half a loaf.

When opening night does arrive, make it as gala as possible, with as much fanfare as you can muster. Have the party as lavish as you can afford, even a little more lavish than you can afford. Your own friendly liquor dealer may be coaxed into a donation of wine, or at least a special low price for it. The actors will be hungry, and the audience also, so nice small homemade sandwiches would be welcome, or canapes and cookies. Those who make them can be thanked publicly for their efforts at the end of the performance.

There will, or course, be many thanks to bestow for all the work that has been done to make the opening night possible. Keep the speeches and thanks brief. Write it all down if you are not a good off-the-cuff speaker, and don't take more than ten minutes for the entire ceremony. But the ceremony is important. If you have any famous guests or local celebrities present, do not overlook them. They like to be introduced. Remember that it is not necessary to have each person being thanked take a personal bow, unless there are very few of them, which is not usual. If you have ten or more, mention their names and their contributions and then ask them all to rise *en masse*, which is very effective.

This ceremony is not the time to make a long speech about your plans or to solicit new members or money. Make it an upbeat occasion for all, especially for your actors and workers, and you will be off to a heart-warming start, with any minor shortcomings in the performance quickly forgotten.

chapter 2

Picking the Play

THE FIRST AND most important step to be taken by those involved in community theatre is picking the play to be presented. Many problems can be avoided if they are foreseen when this choice is made.

For instance, there could be the problem of your playing area. Is it large enough to accommodate the cast the play calls for? Do you have a small proscenium stage (the traditional "box" with its fourth wall open to the audience), or a flexible area which can be used in-the-round (the audience on all sides) or a thrust-stage (the audience on three sides)? Do you have a scenic designer and technicians capable of turning out the set or sets needed? What about the costumes required? Are they modern clothes that your actors can bring from their own wardrobes or must they be specially bought, rented, or designed and made? Do you have the equipment for those special sound effects which some plays need for dramatic or comedic moments? How about your lighting equipment? Some plays are lost without proper mood lighting.

Then there are questions you must answer about the talents of your actors, when picking the play. Can they handle poetic language? Accents? Comedy? Do you have more women than men, as is usual in community theatres?

What are the pros and cons of drama versus comedy? What plays, after all, are available for amateur productions? Current Broadway hits never are. Is the play you are considering too well known to your public? Has there been a film made of it, and will your cast have the problem of trying to live up to the audience's memory of some famous stars in the parts? How difficult will it be to stage the play? How do you judge if a particular play is for your company?

How indeed? A Neil Simon comedy may strike you as a dead-sure winner, but does it fit your actors? That is very important. Despite the recommendation of *Plaza Suite* in the preceding chapter, it needs players with an innate sense of timing and a sharp sense of comedy to play Simon with true success. And not just one or two of them either, but a whole ensemble of them working together. So, in the final analysis, what kind of company do you have? Have you eight or ten stalwarts you can depend upon? Say six women and four men? Or, more likely, seven women and three men? Can you reach out into your community and bring in added talent if and when you need it? Or will you select your play to fit the players you already have?

Perhaps you have someone exceptionally gifted and well liked by your audience who can be the key to your selection. There is almost nothing that delights the audience more than a good vehicle for the actor, professional or amateur, who was "born" to play that part.

On the other hand, although you may have the ideal *Mr. Roberts* and he is insisting on playing it, can you gather together the nineteen men and one girl to make up the cast? Will your playing area accommodate them? Do you have a real comic for Ensign Pulver and a mean old grouch for the Captain? And how will they all fare by comparison to their counterparts in the famous film? *Mr. Roberts*, by Thomas Heggen and Joshua Logan, has become something of a classic and efforts should be made to present it, but the foregoing problems must be taken into consideration.

Similar problems, more or less, apply to Clare Boothe Luce's *The Women*, with its all-female cast of thirty-five. Also, such an oldie is less desirable to present because of the constant showing of the splendid film version on TV late and late-late shows. Nevertheless, it, too, is a classic of its kind, and if you can scare up that many women and have an audience-pleaser who wants to do what is now called "the Rosalind Russell part," it should be done. Mrs. Luce had a keen eye and ear and the wit to make an unsavory but too true-to-life story into a play of considerable warmth and good humor.

But, of course, your male actors may complain if you do *The Women*, as the ladies may if you do *Mr. Roberts*. The nice thing about community theatre is that everybody wants to act. That terrific urge is what makes so many amateur productions exceptionally enjoyable. Every actor has his heart in what he is doing and more than often real ensemble playing is achieved. This is difficult to find

Amateur groups should be open to performing new plays. Above: a production of *The Legend of the Bell Witch*, an original script by Audrey Campbell. *(Picture courtesy of The Nashville Children's Theatre, Nashville, Tenn.)* Costume dramas present their own unique problems. Below: *The Devil's Disciple*. *(Picture courtesy of Waterloo Community Playhouse, Waterloo, Iowa.)*

sometimes in the professional theatre, where actors often seem so intent on making a personal success that thes almosignore thei sellow players. But, of course, that can be the fault of a director who lacks a firm hand. We'll take up that problem, as it affects community theatre, later.

Another problem is the play where the characters have accents, which, for some unknown reason, amateurs frequently choose to ignore. The results can be horrendous. For instance, J.W. Synge's *The Playboy of the Western World*, and Sean O'Casey's *Juno and the Paycock*—great plays, both—should be avoided like the swine flu. Speaking with a true Irish accent seems an impossibility for American actors, even the most professional and most accomplished, and their efforts manage to ruin the poetry and rhythm of the fine works from the Emerald Isle. Sometimes one Irish character in a play can get by, although just recently that fast-rising young actor, John Lithgow, came a cropper, in my estimation, as Matt Burke, the Irish seaman in the Liv Ullman revival of O'Neill's *Anna Christie*, on Broadway. Yet I saw an Equity Library Theatre production of that play (ELT at 102nd Street and Riverside Drive is virtually a New York City "neighborhood community theatre," although the actors are professionals and, of course, Equity members) where Scott Stewart, who is not particularly well-known, was exactly right, accent and all. So, you never know. But an entire cast of Americans speaking with Irish accents? Very difficult, and usually hard on the ears!

The same goes, as far as I am concerned, for a play in any dialect or accent, whether it be French, Russian, or especially Yiddish or Italian. As I said before, one character, even when played with a sort of lop-sided accent, can get away with it, but not a stageful. Maybe, though, I am being too much of a perfectionist for community theatre productions, and maybe your audience won't mind, or may even enjoy, seeing their friends take on a good comedy like *Saturday, Sunday, Monday*, which is about difficulties in an Italian family in Rome. I saw a fine production of this play, which is by Eduard de Felippi, translated into English by Keith Waterhouse and Willis Hall, at the Arena Stage in Washington, D.C. My friend, Dolores Sutton, played the leading role of the beleaguered mother. Dolores is anything but the typical Italian mother type, being young, slim and pretty. But she is a gifted actress, and with her sly sense of comedy she made a real hit in it.

The play had been a success in Italy and London, but had failed miserably on Broadway. I was surprised to find it being done by Zelda Fichandler at her prestigious Arena theatre. She had seen the London production, however, and had liked it very much. Broadway, she decided, could not have seen it done right. Zelda's production was a delightful one, helped mightily by Dolores, whom I call my "closet comedienne" because unless you know her well, she gives the appearance and impression of an actress who would be at her best only in dramatic roles. Anyway, Zelda was right. The play was a small sold-out hit for her, and I enjoyed it mightily.

Later I asked Dolores why the cast spoke with Italian accents when the play is laid in Italy and the characters all are supposed to be speaking Italian.

"That is always a problem," Dolores said. "One wants to give the impression of being an Italian and in our case the director wanted us to speak English voluably and rapidly, as though we were speaking Italian, not with an Italian accent, but with an Italian rhythm of speech. Some of the cast achieved it—she did—and others just couldn't do it and lapsed into various accents, which they deplored. Being a comedy we got away with it. It really was great fun."

It might be fun for your company, too.

Sometimes plays like *Saturday, Sunday, Monday* that do not make it on Broadway become favorites in community and regional theatres. John Patrick, who is known for his often-produced *The Hasty Heart* and *The Teahouse of the August Moon* (which I produced at City Center and also in Mexico, in Spanish, and later in Spanish for a U.S. State Department tour of Latin-America), said that he has made over $400,000 from *The Curious Savages* even though the play did not succeed on Broadway. *The Curious Savages*, by the way, is about a family named Savage, not about aborigines. It is still being given with pleasant regularity, John says.

There are good reasons for a community theatre group to present a play which was not a success in its original production. Some plays—a few of the minor works of Edward Albee and of Tennessee Williams come to mind—are much more effective in the intimacy of a little theatre production than they were in the larger Broadway theatre. And a group which is serious about its work can often bring an intensity to a more or less unknown play which may ferret out new meanings and transmit them to the audience. What could be more creatively satisfying? Besides, it is often more fun to start with a play which is unfamiliar to the actors and to which they

Tennessee Williams is always popular among amateur groups that can handle the Southern drawls and still be understood. Above: *Cat on a Hot Tin Roof. (Picture courtesy of the Dayton Playhouse, Dayton, Ohio.)* Below: The U.S. premiere of *Walsh* by Sharon Pollock was performed by a community theatre group in Iowa. *(Picture courtesy of Waterloo Community Playhouse, Waterloo, Iowa.)*

therefore bring no preconceptions about their characterizations. It allows more leeway to both actors and director.

So don't stick to just the big hits. If a play fails but is picked up by Samuel French, Inc., or The Dramatists Play Service, it has something to offer and should be considered. For instance, a comedy I liked very much, although the New York critics did not, was *The Paisley Convertible*, by Harry Cauley. It has a splendid comedy part for a pretty young woman who plays the leading man's former fiancee. Betsy von Furstenberg played it on Broadway and it was one of the best things she has done. (Betsy is another Ina Claire, but unfortunately plays with roles for them are few and far between these days.) *The Paisley Convertible* was given a whirl on the summer circuit after its untimely closing in New York and it was a "laugh tonic," according to its reviews.

Community theatres have been offering it to their audiences with equally happy results, I am told. It is an easy comedy to do; it has only one set, with that convertible covered in paisley material (hence the title) and there are really good parts for two men and three women. One thing to take into consideration, however, where *The Paisley Convertible* is concerned, as I remarked about the Neil Simon plays, is the ability of your actors to master the timing necessary when doing comedy. There is nothing more embarrassing to amateurs than performing comedy for an audience that doesn't find it funny and doesn't laugh. Worse still, sometimes they laugh at the wrong places. When the actors are playing a tried and true hit and the audience doesn't laugh, it is definitely the fault of the cast and a lack of timing or comedy instinct. This is a major consideration when picking the play your group should do. Onstage lapses (forgotten lines, wrong moves or "pieces of business") are far less obvious in dramas than in comedies, which must be precise and crystal-clear. It is like the difference between playing Liszt and Mozart, where a stray note is overlooked in the former and is as noticeable as the proverbial sore thumb in the latter.

There is a really terrible thing that sometimes happens to amateurs playing a great comedy: they break themselves up! They hear the audience laugh, perhaps for the first time, say on opening night, and natural contagion and lack of professional discipline finds them in an uncontrollable fit of laughter themselves. (This is not the same as the laugh syndrome discussed along with ways of preventing it in the chapter on Directing.) Sometimes they never do get back on an even keel and the evening approaches a catastrophe.

Audiences are not amused and usually become embarrassed for the players.

So, from one viewpoint, drama is safer, especially for a new company with totally inexperienced members. There almost always is more depth to the characters in drama, and that gives the beginner a better chance to submerge himself in the part and with proper direction and rehearsal end up with a creditable performance which the audience will take to heart.

Besides, serious drama should have a place at least now and then on the programs of community theatres because we so seldom see them in New York any more. It is almost impossible for a serious play to make money on Broadway these days, even when it is given good notices by the critics. *The Shadow Box*, for instance, was awarded the Pulitzer Prize and the "Tony" in addition to its glowing reviews, but at this writing is struggling to keep alive and may not recoup its investment. Even I, admiring as I do its fine acting company and the extraordinarily perceptive direction by Gordon Davidson, would not recommend it for an evening out, or for a community theatre audience. It left me extremely depressed with its scene of imminent death on the grounds of a cancer hospital, although Michael Cristofer, the author, is trying to say something like "Life is wonderful; live it up while you have it." Thornton Wilder did it better in *Our Town*, which always leaves me uplifted and inspired to "realize life while you live it—every, every minute," as Emily says in that lovely play.

Equus, on the other hand, is a very serious play and an immensely successful one. It is the first drama to come along in many a moon which continues to sell out into its third year. Of course, it has had the benefit of big names: First Anthony Hopkins; then Richard Burton (what a boost that gave to business! Burton played it for a short while to prepare for the film version which he has now completed); Anthony Perkins has been in and out, and currently is out while Leonard Nimoy, the famous *Star Trek* man, is in. But the strength of the play itself and the spectacularly theatrical way it is presented made its success apparent right from the first night.

Probably it will be a long time before the rights are available for community theatres, but when they are, many companies will present it with varying results, and with and without the controversial nude scene between the neurotic youth and the young girl. The story is told almost like a whodunit, and audiences are as eager as the psychiatrist is to understand why the boy who loved horses suddenly took a steel horseshoe pick and blinded six of them. A play

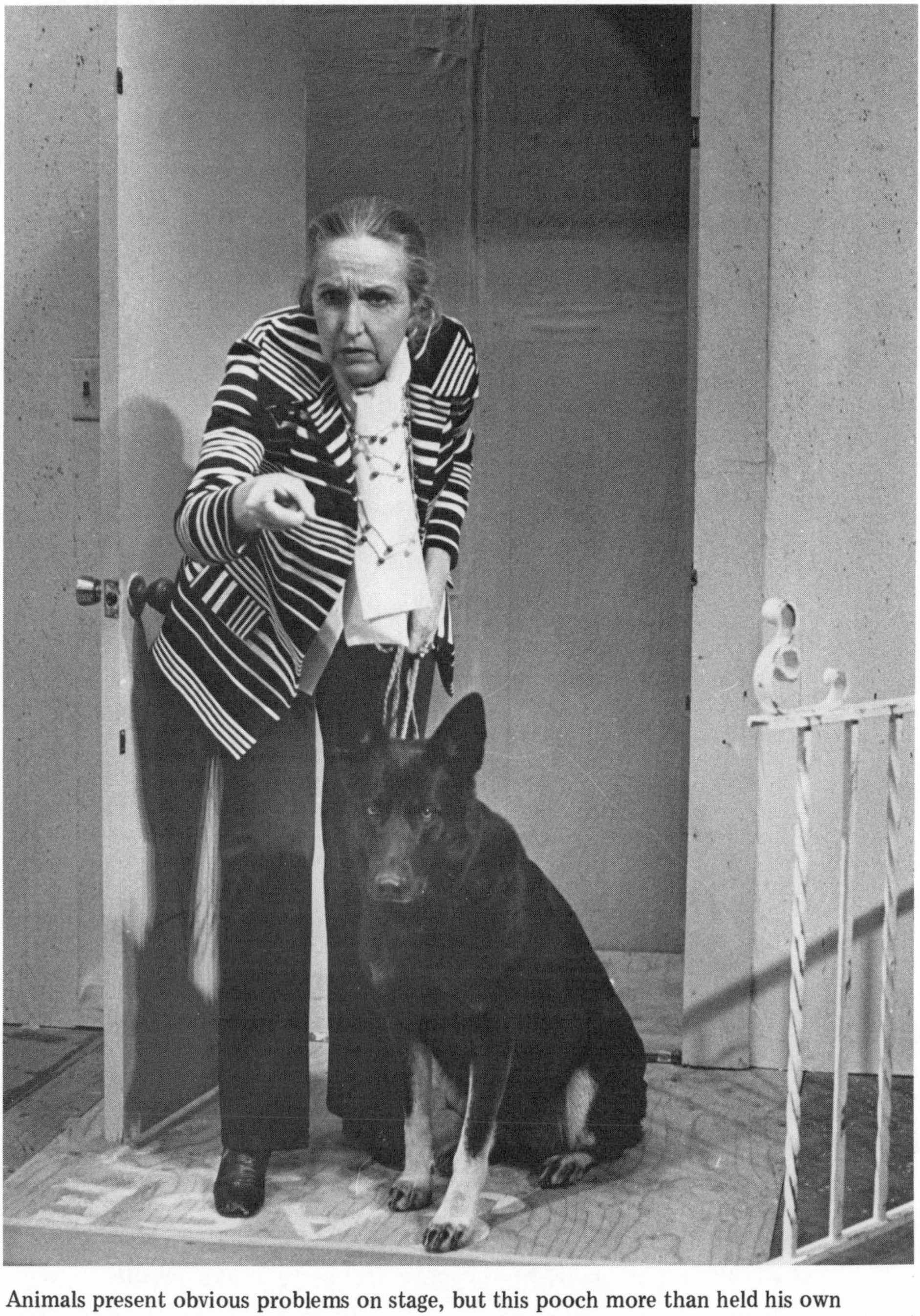

Animals present obvious problems on stage, but this pooch more than held his own with the human actors in a little theatre production of *6 Rms Riv Vu*. *(Picture courtesy of Masquers, Inc. Community Theatre, Manitowoc, Wisc.)*

based on such an inhumanly cruel act would not seem likely to attract the average play-goer, but the direction and entire presentation of *Equus* is so overwhelming—with its boxing arena acting space, its stage bleachers filled with on-lookers, and its fabulously attractive "horses," to say nothing of the tension and suspense created by the playwright—that audiences applaud and cheer and rush to tell their friends to see it without a thought of the subject matter, or even a warning about the nude scene not being something quite appropriate for their aging aunt's birthday celebration.

Another serious, albeit enigmatic, play is Edward Albee's *Seascape*, which had a spine-tingling Broadway performance by Frank Langella, as well as very fine performances by Deborah Kerr and Barry Nelson. With so many important names attached, and respectable reviews, this play should have done well, but it did not. However, it would be interesting for a community company to try it, especially if the group has a gifted costume designer who would like to outfit "the creature from the sea" (played on Broadway by Langella).

Following *Seascape*, Edward Moore's *The Sea Horse* comes to mind. It could be called a serious comedy. It never did get to Broadway, but it was a decided hit off-Broadway. It would have played successfully for a longer period of time had it been presented in a more accessible theatre than one way over on New York's West Side in the forties, and upstairs at that. The play has only two characters and one set, and it is important that the one woman be not just plump but downright fat. It was played originally by Conchita Farley with the man played by the author. So, if you haven't had a part for a long time for that good actress in your company because she has been putting her hand in the cookie boxes too often, tell her to enjoy her double chocolate milkshakes, her creamed potatoes and fettucini Alfredo because you need her for a real roly-poly character. It is a beautiful play, full of humor and seaport charm, but with a serious story for all that. Audiences love it and love that fat girl. (Especially other fat girls!)

Most community theatres are not expected to make money. They are there for people who enjoy theatre-making and theatre-going to have a place where both joys are made possible. To produce nothing but popular works which will assure a full house is rather avoiding the point they are trying to make in the community.

Theatre began in the churches and it has always been a platform for people who are burning to have their ideas and notions, good or awful, brought strikingly and, if possible, startlingly, to the public. George Bernard Shaw told me that he found narrative writing enjoyable and not at all difficult, while playwrighting was exhausting for him. But he wrote many plays, he said, because he felt that the ideas he wanted to express would have more impact when spoken than when read.

"When I stand at the back of a theatre and hear my words being listened to by a packed house, I am rewarded for all the hours, days and months I have spent writing them, and I know the stage is my forum," is the way Shaw put it.

Shaw and those ideas he was so eager to communicate, made a small fortune for us at the New York City Center when we produced his *Misalliance*. It could be equally successful for you, and it is most amusing. We did it as part of a drama season at the City Center on West 55th Street. It ran its allotted two weeks there and was moved to a Broadway theatre where it enjoyed a full season and then continued on tour, bringing a lovely flow of money into our always needy coffers, money needed, by the way, not for our drama company, but to help support our opera and ballet companies. Shaw's *The Devil's Disciple* also was a hit for us and, being a bit of Amercian history, was a play much done by community theatres during the bi-centennial. Our *Devil's Disciple*, starring Maurice Evans, also moved to Broadway for a long run.

Today most young playwrights, with or without ideas, are trying to turn out hits, which translates to comedies, because comedies have a better chance of being produced, they say. Serious plays do not have as much chance. Of course, they are talking about Broadway production.

They are not talking about Joseph Papp, with his myriad of theatre spaces and plenty of subsidy, to say nothing of his fortune-making *A Chorus Line*. Papp takes experimental and serious plays and works them out at one of those spaces in his huge Public Theatre on Lafayette Street. If the play looks good, Papp then puts it in one of the off-Broadway theatres in his building and opens it to the critics and the public. If they like it, the show moves uptown to Broadway. Such was Papp's method in the discovery and mounting of the plays of David Rabe, Jason Miller, Ntozaki Shange and others. Three of Rabe's plays came to Broadway (the Vivien Beaumont Theatre at Lincoln Center is considered a Broadway house). They were *Sticks and Bones, The Basic Training of*

When deciding whether or not to do a play like *A Taste of Honey* (above), a community theatre must consider the sensitivities of its particular audience. *(Picture courtesy of Harrisburg Community Theatre, Harrisburg, Pa.)* Some older plays like *Biography* (below), written in the 1930s by S. N. Behrman, are not at all dated, and well worth doing. *(Picture courtesy Henderson Little Theatre, Henderson, N.C.)*

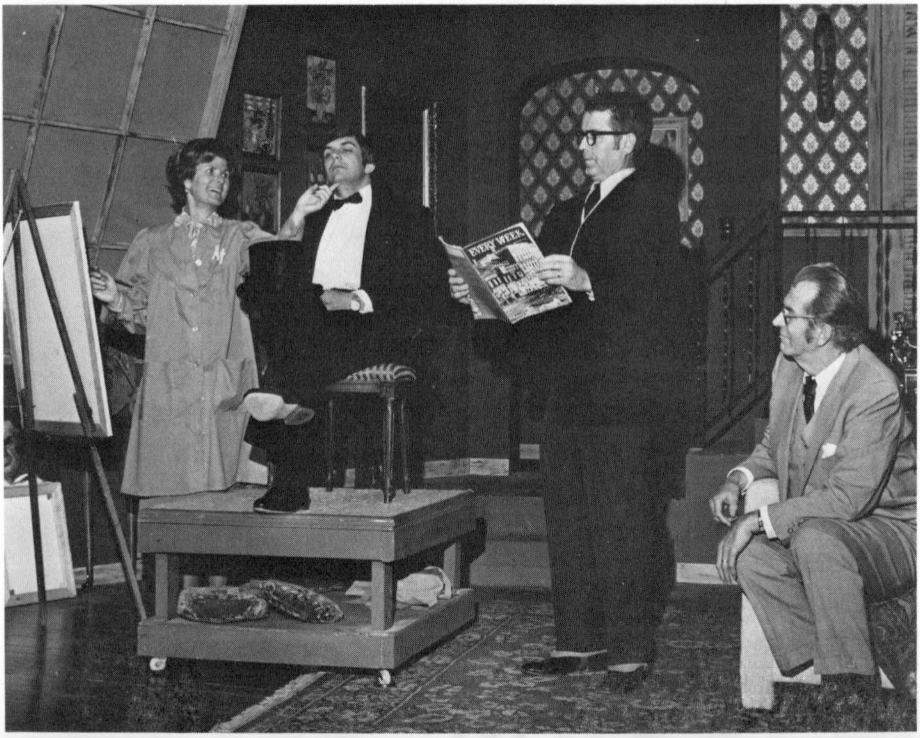

Pavlo Hummel, and *The Boom-Boom Room*; his *Streamers* had a long run at the off-Broadway theatre in Lincoln Center, the Mitzi Newhouse.

Jason Miller's *That Championship Season* made history both down on Lafayette Street, and on Broadway, and Ms. Shange's *For Colored Girls Who Have Considered Suicide/When the Rainbow Is Enuf* currently is a success at the Booth Theatre. All of these plays are interesting ones for the community theatre. None of Rabe's plays, I must add, are family fare, but he is an exciting writer with provocative ideas.

Fortunately, it is not a life and death matter to most community theatres if one of the plays selected does not attract a large public, so it is possible to present, for instance, the lesser works of Tennessee Williams, as well as his classic money-makers. After all, Williams is our finest poetic playwright living today, and he has splendid ideas and beautiful words. His play *The Rose Tattoo* is a favorite of mine in spite of its calling for Italian accents in the two leading roles. Its setting is a bit complicated for small theatres, and a sensitive background music score is an important asset, but with two players who understand Williams's humor and who can make a presentable stab at that Italian accent, it can be a delight and a real contribution to any theatre group's program. I like most of his one act plays, too, and suggest *27 Wagons Full of Cotton* and *The Case of the Crushed Petunias* as community theatre candidates for entertaining and enlightening performances.

One act plays, in fact, should be a staple of community theatre production. They have many advantages. Usually they have small casts and one set. Sometimes they call for no set at all, just good lighting, props and a chair or two. They permit a director and his actors to concentrate on the action within a short time period. Then, too, inexperienced actors who invariably have difficulty memorizing their lines, will welcome the shorter parts.

There are many one-act plays by great writers suitable for community theatre. Shaw, for instance, has written some that are enchanting. So has Thornton Wilder. Then there is Edward Albee's *The Zoo Story*, Arthur Miller's *A View From the Bridge* (later expanded to a full-length play but still available to little theatre groups as a one-acter) and Murray Schisgall's *The Tiger*. Some of Pinter's short plays are fascinating, but may be both too enigmatic and too depressing for community theatre audiences.

If you are putting together an evening of short plays, it is important that you chose works that are compatible with each other and build as the program progresses, with the one you feel is the strongest coming at the end. An audience is always eager to laugh, which is why they grasp at the slightest mishap to giggle or guffaw, so if you are doing two serious plays and a comedy, make the comedy your finale. As the saying goes, "Always leave them laughing."

Getting back to serious full-length plays, there is always Shakespeare. But I am informed that he is close to impossible for community players to memorize and perform. Well, he is difficult for professionals, too. His lines should be spoken, as Hamlet tells the players, "trippingly on the tongue," which is an attribute seemingly beyond many American actors. That is not because they are inept, but because the English language is so indifferently spoken by most of us, and so beautifully spoken by the educated Englishman. Even amateur productions of the Bard's works when done in his native land are enjoyable because they are such a pleasure to listen to, and when they are done at Stratford-on-Avon or by the National Company or the Old Vic in London, they are often overwhelmingly magnificent. I was fortunate enough to see Richard Burton in his early days at the Old Vic play *Coriolanus*; and that difficult tragedy, so seldom done in our country, and his performance, are unforgettable.

However, Shakespeare is done by us, and successfully, too. Joseph Papp's Shakespeare-in-the-Park company has presented virtually all of his works in various American accents and with various results. Some of the tragedies have been embarrassing, but all of the comedies have been treats. His early outdoor production of *The Taming of the Shrew* made me a convert to his dream of "Shakespeare for everybody, for free!" How far he has come since those days.

So, while Shakespeare is difficult and we don't speak lines "trippingly on the tongue," perhaps some of his more popular works—or scenes from them—should be undertaken by the community theatres that have players who would enjoy the challenge and who can remember the lines. The latter can be done by laymen if the will is present. I knew a newspaperman who had committed almost the entire *Hamlet* to memory because of his love for "those magnificent words," and I know many people whose only connection with the professional theatre is to buy a ticket to enter one, who delight in reciting great chunks of the better-known scenes. I'd suggest a comedy to start—say that never-failing *The Taming of the Shrew* if your group has the ambition to put on Shakespeare.

Equally as adventuresome as presenting Shakespeare is putting on a new work. Perhaps you have an aspiring playwright, or even an experienced one, in your community whose ideas cannot find a professional platform. There is a playwright in Florida who sends me very nice plays with good ideas which I keep saying are not ready for Broadway but deserve a showing, perhaps in her own community. She replies that her local theatre people say they cannot take a chance on plays that have not already been given in New York. That is a pity, but things are changing. The many regional theatres scattered from coast-to-coast are now eager for good new plays. Some of them have had an original production go to Broadway, giving them a boost in prestige as well as income, and now they'd all like to follow suit. It could happen to a community theatre, too. So why not take a flyer now and then?

On the other hand, a new play worth the back-breaking work it takes to bring it to a successful performance in the regional theatre, the Broadway theatre or the community theatre, is as rare as the proverbial pearl in the oyster, and you may never, never find one. If you do, however, and decide to go ahead with it, you must be prepared for unexpected difficulties. Unlike the plays you select from the catalogues, you will have no guide lines. You will not have the benefit of a script that has been written and rewritten, rehearsed and rerehearsed, played and replayed until it is as flawless as that particular playwright's original brainchild could be made by the many talents that have polished it. In my opinion, a play fresh from the typewriter is only about half of the hit you see on opening night. The other half has been added to it by the director, the actors, the scenic and costume designers, the producer, the press agent, all the artists and technicians involved. The director and the actors often change lines for the better and add those "pieces of business" which bring laughter, and the author has no complaint as a rule. No one takes a cut of his royalties, or even shares in his plaudits. However, the stage manager carefully notes all the changes and additions, bits of business and the director's carefully worked-out crosses, positions, exits and entrances. Thus the script from which you will probably be working is a virtual blue-print of the play, which need only be carefully observed and followed.

But if you do have the good fortune to come across a virgin play which you can fall hopelessly in love with, by all means do it. Struggle through all the problems that probably will arise, and win or lose you will find it has been worth the effort. You will have learned what goes into bringing about that effortless grace with which a hit play seems to be done and you will have the satisfaction of having made a noble effort in the same direction.

Not finding that exceptional play, you will stick with the tried and true, so please remember the fundamentals: select the play which fits your players, your acting space, and your public, and for which you have the other requisite talents and materials.

If you need advice at any time, you can always write or call Samuel French, Inc., or the Dramatists Play Service. These two great and helpful companies specialize in service to community theatre groups. They control the rights to the majority of the thousands of contemporary plays which make up the programs of community theatres from coast to coast. They will help you select your play, should you ask them, and then they will furnish you not only with sufficient scripts for your company but with any tapes that are needed for special music or sound effects. If by chance a play you would like to do is not in their libraries, they will tell you where you can locate it. Here are the addresses of both:

Samuel French, Inc.
25 West 45th Street
New York, N.Y. 10036
Telephone: 582-4700 (212)

Dramatists Play Service, Inc.,
440 Park Avenue,
New York, N.Y. 10016
Telephone: 683-8960 (212)

Following is a list of those who control rights and provide scripts for the plays suggested in this chapter:

The Neil Simon plays
  Samuel French, Inc.,

Mr. Roberts
  Samuel French, Inc.

Saturday, Sunday, Monday
  Samuel French, Inc.

The Women
  Dramatists Play Service, Inc.

When picking the play, such advantages as a small cast (fewer problems with rehearsal schedules) and one simple set, as is the case with *Who's Afraid of Virginia Woolf?* may be decisive factors. *(Picture courtesy of Long Island Studio Theatre of Lindenhurst, N.Y.)*

The John Patrick plays
Steven Sultan, c/o International Creative Management,
40 West 57th St., New York, N.Y. 10019
Tel: 556-5600 (212)

The Paisley Convertible
Samuel French, Inc.

Equus
Kermit Bloomgarden Estate, 275 Central Park West,
New York, N.Y. 10024
Tel: 787-5481

Seascape
Dramatists Play Service, Inc.

The Sea Horse
James T. White & Co., 1700 State Highway #3,
Clifton, N.J. 07013
Tel: 773-9300 (201)

The David Rabe plays
Ellen Neuwald, 905 West End Avenue, New York, N.Y. 10025
Tel: 663-1586

That Championship Season
Dramatists Play Service, Inc.

For Colored Girls Who Have
J. Lloyd Grant, 414 Ave. of the Americas, New York, N.Y. 10019
Tel: 688-4112

The Tennessee Williams plays
Dramatists Play Service, Inc.

The George Bernard Shaw plays
The Society of Authors, 84 Drayton Gardens, London, S.W. 10, England.

chapter 3

The Musical

WHEN YOU AND your company decide you need a change, or would like to take a flyer, an operetta or musical can give you a fine chance to try new wings. Actually it is my opinion that a musical has a better chance of being that big hit a community theatre group is always looking for, given the proper basic material and attractive players, than most straight plays. You need a good basic story to begin with, which is the book, or the play-part, but then you have the added elements of the music and the dance, either of which, or both, if capably done, can put the show over with a gusto which will leave your audience breathless with delight.

Just as in selecting a straight play, however, you must avoid pitfalls and catastrophe by choosing the musical with great care. Like the play without music, it must suit your audience and fit your company. Do you have good dancers or at least players who move well and can be taught to dance? How about singers? Of course, everyone thinks he can sing and has sung in school or in church, and in the bathroom, but that can be a problem for you. Is there a pillar of your company who will insist on having the leading role even though he can't carry a tune? Be firm. Turn him down, or he will be an embarrassment to you and your audience, which will include his suffering wife and children. A less gifted member of your company with a voice that will stay on pitch will add to rather than detract from your chances for a hit.

How about your playing area? If it is a dancing show, considerable space is needed. Are the costumes elaborate and costly? Can you rent them? Will that be too expensive? Can they be made locally? Will your set designer and your builders be able to produce the colorful scenery called for? Do you have sufficient lighting equipment? Musicals are generally brightly lighted and call for that all-important follow-spot. Often sound equipment is needed. Do you have it? Can you get it? Most important, do you have someone in your group who knows how to handle it?

All these factors are important to ponder before you make your decision. Just about every musical involves all of them. Some musicals involve more.

Deciding about the music is very important. Will you need an orchestra? Or will one or two pianos, perhaps with percussion added, provide a satisfactory accompaniment? If you believe an orchestra is necessary, can one be locally assembled? How about the conductor? Before making another move, you must think about that. In my opinion, the person you choose will be the key to your success of failure. Select someone who is more than just a good musician who offers to conduct. You must have someone who is a real musical director. (Leopold Stokowski, who formed and led the New York City Center Symphony for several years before Leonard Bernstein took over, insisted upon being called the "music director," not the "musical director," as is the custom. "The director himself is not musical," he explained. "He directs the music. Hence he is a music director, not a musical director.") In the case of the conductor of a musical, however, I prefer the usual term, "musical director," because whoever leads the music actually leads the entire show. I have seen a pretty good musical destroyed by an inept conductor and I have seen a less good one salvaged by a great leader.

If you decide on one or two pianos to furnish the music, the same thing holds true. Whoever leads the music must be not merely a fine pianist but someone with an innate sense of theatre timing and a flair for musical effects, or what is known as the ability to "put a period" at the end of a number, which is the pit musicians' way of saying having the knack of bringing the music and the song or dance to a simultaneous climax which will arouse spontaneous applause from the audience. Many a singer and dancer has been left high and dry by a sloppy musical ending which was too late, or too early, or just plain dull.

If you do not have, or cannot find, the right person for this all-important position, I suggest you postpone your musical until you do.

But taking for granted that you can find such a gem, then turn your attention to the problem of finding a good dance director. Dances are important to most musicals. A good dance director is essential because even amateurs with limited dancing experience

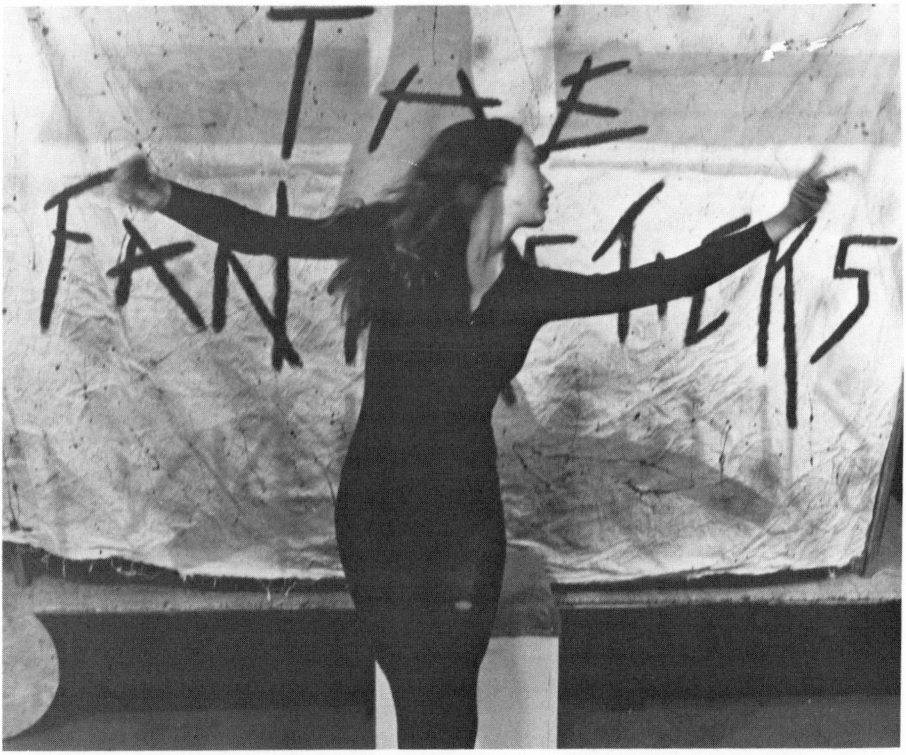

Not all musicals have to be elaborate. If the talent is there, just about any group can put on a simple one like *The Fantasticks. (Pictures courtesy of Long Island Studio Theatre of Lindenhurst, N.Y.)*

can be made to look pretty good by a drill master who knows what he is doing, and with the musical help of that conductor who will "put a period" to the dance numbers.

Talented choral directors also can work semi-miracles with mediocre singers. Church or school choir masters are often pressed into service by community theatre groups with excellent results. While they cannot improve the quality of the voices, they can train them to begin and finish together, which is a big help when you're doing *South Pacific* and want "There's Nothing Like a Dame" to make its usual smash hit.

But I wouldn't recommend *South Pacific* as a starter. Something small and tuneful, like *The Fantasticks*, would be safer. That charming little musical, now in its tenth year off-Broadway in Greenwich Village, and still going strong, is almost fool-proof. It has a small cast, there are no big dance numbers, and the really lovely songs can be sung by just about anyone who claims to be a singer. The set is simple, too, and so is the story. You really have to be running in bad luck on all counts if you don't succeed with *The Fantasticks*.

In a different vein, Lehar's *The Merry Widow* has been done by small companies and is another musical that is difficult to spoil. The score, which just about everyone knows by heart, is not only one of the loveliest of all the light operas, but it is eminently singable. There are several versions of the book, but the one which Tams Witmark, the company which controls the rights to hundreds of musicals, can furnish, along with all the necessary musical parts, is excellent. With a charming soprano for the widow, a dashing Prince Danilo, and amusing character men and women, all with pretty nice voices, and all able to move well, you just can't miss, even if you cannot muster a large dancing chorus. There are always pretty girls available to a community theatre group who enjoy trying their luck at doing a rousing "Can-Can"! Two pianos do nicely, if well played, and you have that essentially gifted leader, but the last time I saw *The Merry Widow* put on by a community group, a small orchestra had been put together by local amateur musicians, and they did just fine.

After you decide upon the musical you will do, and have found your musical director, stage director, dance director and any other leaders needed, gather up your basic company of players and have them read through the book. Some exceptional virtuosity may turn up in your own company.

As you go along, during the reading, you will be able to judge just how much dancing is needed with how many dancers, and if your playing area is adequate and how it can best be utilized. You will get a feeling of the rhythm of the entire show and will know, which is very important, if the dialogue holds up or needs slight cuts or even some alteration for your particular audience. This is too often the case with some of the oldies, which generally have scores far superior to the books. As your players read the parts which you have distributed randomly, with the warning that they well may not play the part they are reading, that virtuosity I mentioned may turn up. In any case they all will be learning what will be expected of them and you will be getting a good overall idea of what problems, if any, you face.

If all goes well and your casting is soon complete, a time table is agreed upon: so many hours, or days, or weeks for each director—musical, dance, etc.—with the stage director receiving the lion's share. When the time for run-throughs is reached, the stage director will be in complete charge and will co-ordinate everyone's work into, hopefully, a smooth, fast-moving performance. The dance director usually helps the stage director at this time, working out the movement of the players as they go into and out of their numbers, both songs and dances. This is a good time to decide about encores. It will be pretty evident by this time, from the reactions of all concerned, which numbers will be or have a good chance of being show-stoppers and it is a good idea to be prepared with a sort of coda or short repeat, perhaps of the finale or last several bars of the music. In *The Merry Widow,* for instance, both "Girls, Girls, Girls," (sung and danced by a male chorus) and the "Can-Can" done with lots of pizzazz, will bring the house down.

Recently the Community Theatre in New Milford, Connecticut, took what for them was a daring and sophisticated step: they presented a new version, in English, of Rossini's opera, *Cenerentala*, called *Cinderella in Italy*. It was presented primarily for children, but the evening I was present, while I saw a few children present, mostly I saw a happy houseful of grown-ups, laughing and applauding the familiar Italian music and delighted to have the beloved story conveyed to them in a language they could understand. The translation and conception of the book is the work of Elizabeth McCormick, who also directed the production. The arrangement of the music and the English lyrics are by Dianys Ries. *Cinderella in Italy* was such a success in New Milford that the Southeast Players in Brewster, N.Y., a community theatre group

There are reasons for doing such much-performed favorites as *South Pacific* (above) and lesser done musicals like *The Me Nobody Knows* (below). *(Picture above courtesy of Des Moines Community Playhouse, Des Moines, Iowa. Picture below courtesy of Lincoln Community Playhouse, Lincoln, Neb.)*

which is part of the Southeast Museum in that town, also decided to present it, and with the same success.

One thing that was important about the New Milford success of an original work by local authors (Miss McCormick lives in nearby Danbury and Miss Ries in Redding) was that it gave the group the courage to try other new works, as well as to plan a "big" musical, Sigmund Romberg's *New Moon*, for their next production. They have a fairly small, well-knit group, but can count on as many as forty talented neighbors to make up the required large cast. However, they probably will engage a professional stage director, which, in my opinion, will eliminate many headaches. The musical director they had for *Cinderella in Italy*, which, by the way, was given with two pianos and taped "interlude" orchestral music, was excellent, and undoubtedly he will conduct the small orchestra they hope to corral locally. *New Moon* has a plethora of scenery, but the New Milford company has a designer who believes he can manage with a "unit set," platforms, and changes of light.

A very short time ago musicals had multiple sets which required the stage hands to make quick changes while dance or song numbers were being done before the curtain or traveller (a curtain which travels from side to side of the stage) in "one," as the forestage is called. Today scenic designers are using their utmost ingenuity to keep the action and the sets themselves moving without interruption, and they are succeeding admirably. Two recent hit musicals, *I Love My Wife* and *Annie*, are prime examples of this new development in scene designing. *I Love My Wife* even keeps its four musicians on stage as part of the decor and action. This four character musical, by the way, with its titillating but innocent plot about changing sexual mores in Trenton, N.J., will be as popular with community players as *The Fantasticks* when it becomes available, but you can be sure that will not happen for some time. *Annie* is another family show which, while more cumbersome scenically and difficult to stage smoothly, will one day soon become what is known in show biz as a "standard."

The costumes for both these musicals do not pose problems, even though *Annie* is a "period piece," the period being the early Roosevelt (FDR) years. There are plenty of nice suits and dresses from those days that will still be hanging in grandma and grandpa's put-away closets when you get to stage it, and the children's clothes can easily be made. *I Love My Wife* is modern, 1977, and the characters—particularly the "square" couple—can just open their own closets.

While on the subject of costumes, I'd like to suggest that period outfits for your leading man, who may be playing a prince, a general, a white-tie-and-tails society man, or such, be bought or rented. Made-on-the-premises costumes for men tend to be poorly cut and put together, with a "homemade" look which gives your handsomest and best built player an untidy if not ludicrous appearance, accompanied by a self-conscious feeling of ill-ease on his part. Renting is expensive but worth it sometimes. On the other hand, if you can buy the necessary outfit, that is still better, for it is much cheaper in the long run. With the addition or subtraction of braid, buttons, medals, epaulets, and such, many changes can be made to suit various characters. Thrift shops are good sources of inexpensive but good quality clothes, especially women's evening gowns and negligees, and sometimes good-looking dinner jackets for men.

With so many costumes to keep track of when doing a musical, it is imperative that a wardrobe mistress be appointed. She will be the custodian of all the costumes and accessories, and will be responsible for their appearance and availability. If the costumes are being made on the premises, she will keep track of the progress being made in getting them ready in time. There really is no excuse for the almost never-failing last minute rush to have costumes ready on time, with pieces of outfits or whole costumes missing for the dress rehearsal, but it happens all the time, even in the professional theatre. It is something that gives producers and directors migraines, to say nothing of the frustration of the player who finds herself lacking that all-important grand finale gown, with its unmanageable train.

When *My Fair Lady* had its first night out-of-town, the costumes were late in arriving, and then it was discovered that all those for the dancers were too tight or too binding to move in! A team of seamstresses let out and basted up the originals for the opening, but a whole new set had to be redesigned and made for New York. The dancers must have their comfort, but it is also important that their costumes fit well, or they will look sloppy and the line and elegance of the dance itself will be marred.

Especially attractive costuming for a soloist or a chorus can be a great help in putting over a song or dance number, especially in amateur productions. The appearance, precision, grace and high spirits of dancers can usually overcome technical lapses to a great degree. There is also the uniformity of a line to be considered. It is a good idea to try to cast girl dancers of approximately the same

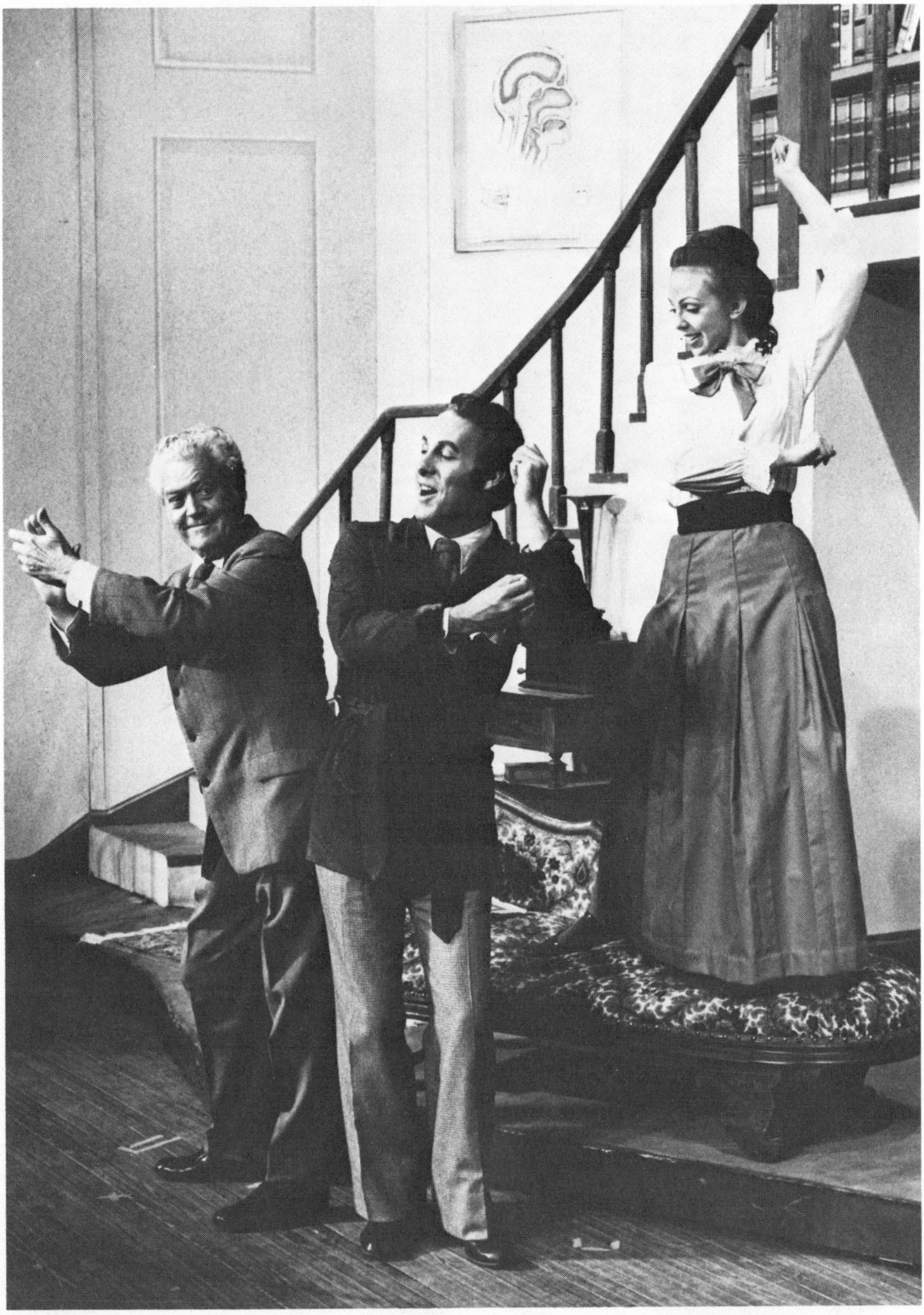

Check out whether your people can handle the accents before trying *My Fair Lady.* *(Picture courtesy of Theatre Memphis, Memphis, Tenn.)*

Rima (above) was an original musical based on *Green Mansions.* *(Picture courtesy of Wyandotte Community Theatre, Allen Park, Mich.)* A most ambitious undertaking for an amateur group is *Candide* (below). *(Picture courtesy Spokane Civic Theatre, Spokane, Wash.)*

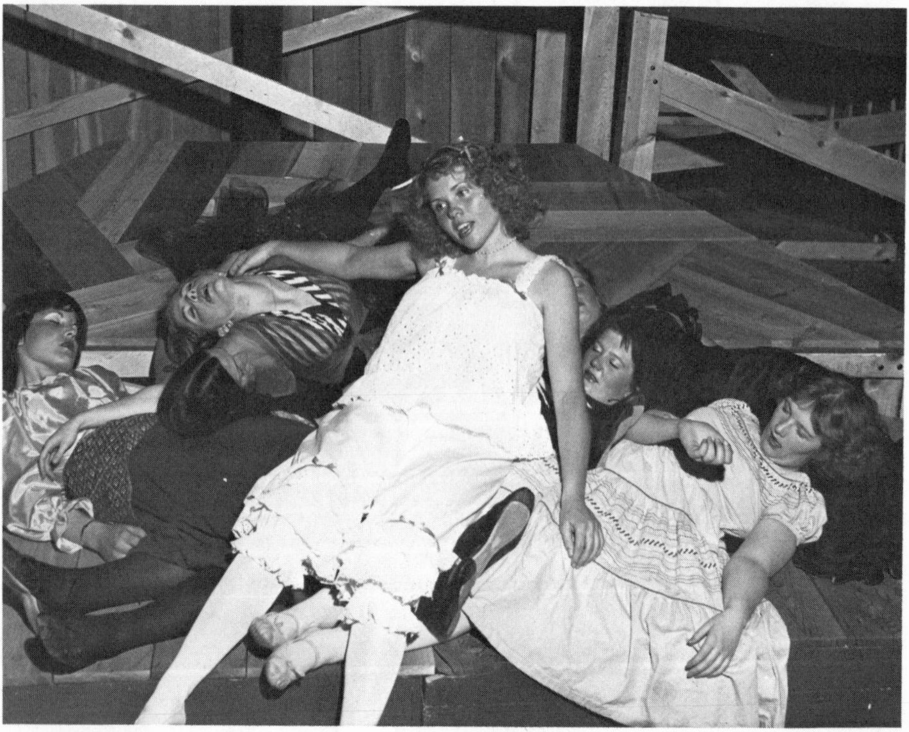

height and build. It doesn't seem to matter so much with the boys. In fact, that ungainly tall fellow with the big grin may just turn out to be the hit of the number, or it could be the small fellow on the end, who is a bit too plump. But the girls do better if they are pretty and spritely and make up a pleasingly uniform line, which is not difficult to achieve when you are using only four or six girls.

A revue, like a program of one act plays, is easier to put together then a musical. A revue has no plot or story line, and consists of humorous skits or sketches, and song or dance numbers, each of which can be rehearsed separately and staged by more than one director. Broadway has not seen a successful revue in a long time, but there were many of them produced in the thirties and forties, the best remembered being by Arthur Schwartz and Howard Dietz, including *The Band Wagon, At Home Abroad* and *Inside U.S.A.* Then there was Charles Gaynor's *Lend an Ear*, which introduced and made a star of Carol Channing, and the perennial *Best Faces* of Leonard Sillman. Mr. Sillman is currently putting together *The Best of Best Faces*, so maybe Broadway will get another good revue soon. In the meantime, community theatre groups would have a difficult time reproducing any of the aforementioned successes, because the rights and materials necessary are not easily available. Chappell & Company, of 810 Seventh Avenue, New York City, 10019, (Tel: 212-399-7100) control most of the music and can be very helpful about locating other material if you want to make an effort in the direction of one of these celebrated revues. Most groups, however, put together their own revues, using standard music numbers and short humorous plays, or "homemade" satirical sketches.

Combining words, music and dance into a beguiling entertainment seems more difficult than staging a play, but it also is great fun if you make the proper decisions and lay out the work to be done well in advance. And the ultimate reward is a delighted audience on opening night.

Following is a list of those who control rights and sometimes provide music for three of the works suggested in this chapter.

The Fantasticks
Music Theatre, Inc., 119 West 57th Street, New York, N.Y.
Tel: 975-6841 (212)

The Merry Widow
Tams Witmark, 757 Third Avenue, New York, N.Y. 10017
Tel: MU 8-2525 (212)

South Pacific

Rodgers and Hammerstein Music Library, 598 Madison Avenue, New York City, 10022
Tel: 486-7378 (212)

Most of the good theatre pieces with music are controlled by the above companies. Samuel French and Dramatists Play Service also have less well-known works listed in their catalogue. Costumes are available from Eaves Costume Company, 423 W. 55th Street, New York City, 10019. Tel: (212) 757-3730.

Some musicals, like *Jacques Brel Is Alive and Well and Living in Paris,* can be done without any scenery or costuming whatever. All it takes is enthusiasm and talent. *(Picture courtesy Long Island Studio Theatre, Lindenhurst, N.Y.)*

chapter 4

Directing

THE ART OF DIRECTING a stage production is comparatively new in the 2400 year history of western theatre. It is recorded that Aeschylus wrote some ninety plays, winning first prize in the Athenium competition of tragic drama more than twenty times (finally being defeated by Sophocles), but there is no mention of anyone who was the guiding force in seeing to it that the plays were properly mounted and acted. In fact, there is no reference anywhere to stage direction for Shakespeare's plays or for any of the famous Restoration comedies. In the nineteenth century a "stage manager" is given a line or two for having "been of assistance" to the actors "surrounding" a star player who evidently needed no guidance and probably accepted none if offered.

The playwright and the leading actors who captured the public's fancy dominated the American theatre through the opening decade of our century as well. The first time stage direction seems to have attracted any particular attention was when David Belasco's press agent placed a series of articles on the drama calling attention to Mr. Belasco's particular approach to staging his productions and his insistence on "realism" and "naturalistic" acting. The plays Mr. Belasco directed and produced were sucessful, his actors' "naturalistic" work was praised, and his own "realism" in stage direction was given due credit.

When George Abbott directed Jed Harris's production of the fabled *Broadway* and later his *Coquette*, in the 1920's, Mr. Abbott's direction was highly praised for its contribution to their success. Since then the stage director has been given more and more importance. Just as we read about "bankable" stars these days, we know there are "bankable" stage directors whose participation in a theatre production is the magnet that draws the financial backing.

(Mike Nichols seems to head the list.) So today the stage director has come into his own.

This is particularly true in the amateur theatre where the director is a key force and has a vital role because he is surrounded by comparatively inexperienced workers in all departments. He must be the autonomous head man—or woman—of the production, the undisputed leader, guide, teacher and diplomat of the company. He must assume the responsibility not only for the eventual acting quality, but for overseeing the myriad details that are involved in bringing any play from the printed page or manuscript to a live and engrossing production.

If your company is fortunate enough to have a number of directors or members who wish to be directors, pick one who seems best fitted to the type of play that has been selected. The quiet, analytical school teacher who has made a success of *A Doll's House* might be less at home and therefore less successful directing *Room Service*, or any of that class of fast-moving situation comedy.

When the director has been appointed, the proper staff for him must be assembled. Perhaps a producer also has been named who will serve as supervisor, trouble-shooter and aide in holding everything together. Some theatres have a permanent staff, but more often the director selects his own team of designers, lighting and sound people, the all-important stage manager, and an alert script boy or girl. This last named is an important addition to any production group, for he or she can relieve both the director and the stage manager of the necessity of "holding the book" and prompting the actors once the scripts are out of their hands. Nothing wastes more rehearsal time than trying to find the place in the script where someone has "gone up." The director has long since had the script out of his hands, and usually the stage manager is so busy writing up the notes he has taken from the director that the action of the play has passed him by and he is as lost as the actor. I've had a stage manager look up and ask, "What scene are we in?" But the person appointed to be "on the book" is following every word, and at a glance or a gesture from the blank-eyed player, he can instantly supply the elusive word or line. This same person can be the prompter in the wings on opening night and during subsequent performances. Then, too, this makes another important job for someone anxious to be part of the production.

Not as important, however, as the stage manager. He is the director's right hand. He should be capable of taking over the direction, should a calamity happen, or should the director simply

Positioning players for a particularly dramatic scene is one of the most important parts of directing. This becomes obvious with such classics as *Ah, Wilderness* by Eugene O'Neill (right) and *Hay Fever* by Noel Coward (below). *(Pictures courtesy of Studio Playhouse, Upper Montclair, N.J.)*

need to miss a rehearsal or two. The stage manager keeps track of everything the director "sets" as rehearsals progress, making countless notes on the margin and in the "master script," such as "Father goes left stage to left end of sofa," or "Father raises voice angrily on this line." But more of his work later.

After the director has selected his staff, he starts the auditions. These should be open to outsiders in order to lure more players to the company. There never can be too many actors from which to choose. The director and stage manager, along with the producer and the casting committee, if there is one, meet with the applicants, take particular note of their appearances, talk with them about their experience and background, and in general decide which ones should be considered. Typecasting is useful to start with. The actors should look the part, and be the correct age, or close to it. It is disconcerting for the audience to see a teenager wearing a white wig and make-up wrinkles while impersonating an aging banker or a loveable old handyman.

However, sometimes the other way round is not too bad, as ages go. A really talented lady in the company who is in her early thirties, but who looks in her teens, can often get away with playing a youngster. And a slim fortyish man can play a college man, and should be so cast if he is one of your public's favorites.

But don't do this sort of casting of unknowns without extensive tests. In fact, all the unknowns need careful examination. Still, if someone new comes in who looks exactly right, and everyone agrees he or she would be great in the part, give him some real help by letting him study the script at home before a reading. The director should discuss the character with the actor and provide a detailed description, if possible, of how he sees the part being played. Then when he returns for the reading, have one of the better actors of the company read the scene with him. Even for professionals it is difficult to give some semblance of a performance at an audition when the stage manager is reading the cue lines in the usual expressionless or exaggerated way stage managers have. For newcomers to amateur theatre, it is even harder.

When I say type-casting is useful in choosing the actors, I don't mean the director should find a counterpart in personality. There is nothing deadlier when casting a comedy, for instance, than selecting someone you think is rather boring in real life to play a role which is supposed to be that of a boring character. That person in the play undoubtedly is used as a butt for comedy lines. He is what we call a "straight man," and a good one is worth his weight in diamonds. The "straight man" is aware of the comedy situations he finds himself in, and it is his reaction to a line or piece of business which brings the laugh, as much as the witty or amusing line itself. Pick someone with an unusual personality or appearance to play that dull insurance man, and with the proper direction he will do well. Yes, matching a character's personality can be disastrous. But "looking the part" can nevertheless be a plus for casting.

As a director, you will be aware of the fact that by the time your group has done a few plays, actors will have come and actors will have gone, but there will be a nucleus of talented people who hang in there and will in effect form a sort of repertory company. You will have seen enough of these people in action—readings, improvisations and actual plays—to have formed an opinion of each of them. You will have some idea of their capabilities, of their ranges and limitations. There is nothing wrong with drawing upon this knowledge when you are casting for a play. The only thing to be wary of is easy pigeonholing. Just because Jane played a frowsy frump in the last play doesn't mean she can't handle the fashion model part in this one; and John may have gotten a lot of laughs his last time out, but that doesn't mean he lacks the sensitivity for serious drama. Judge the person by his or her capabilities, not so much by what they have done as by what your experience with them tells you they have the talent to do.

This sort of background knowledge will also help prevent future problems at the casting stage. Every cast of every play, and the backstage people and the director as well, have their share of personality conflicts. Putting on a play is both an extremely intense and an artificial situation. The strain is great and the best of relationships become tense as opening night draws closer. If there are those in the cast, or among the back-up people, who don't get along with each other, it can lead to a disaster. The time to prevent such a disaster, inasmuch as the director is aware of such feelings, is when the play is being cast. Do not cast people who don't like each other. Do not cast people who clash. Try to avoid having husbands and wives in the same plays. (They almost always bring their marital stresses on the set with them.)

It would seem obvious that the wise director would not cast people who have been married to each other but are now divorced in the same play. One director we know violated this rule in an amateur production of Ionesco's *The Bald Soprano*. This one-act play, a fine and hilarious example of Theatre of the Absurd, features dialogue which is really a stringing together of *non se-*

quiturs. At the dress rehearsal, the former mates interrupted the performance with a screaming argument consisting of insults hurled back and forth at each other. The rest of the cast was appalled, the director in despair. But the guests who had been invited to the dress rehearsal did not know that any brouhaha had taken place. They thought that the argument was part of the dialogue of the play. Their loudest applause was reserved for the couple, and later on some of them complimented the pair on the "authenticity" of their performances.

There is a postscript to this incident. On opening night the woman involved—her name was Helen—received a large bouquet of flowers backstage just before the play began. The other women in the cast, much impressed, asked her who had sent them and what the card which came with them said. Before she could answer, her hostile ex-husband piped up: "To Helen; from Helen!" he sneered. And on that note the show had to go on.

The lesson is obvious. Hostile relationships do not improve on stage. If possible, avoid the problem in advance when casting.

Another type of twosome to avoid when casting is the duo engaging in an affair although one or both may be married to someone else. These people will be using the rehearsal situation as a cover-up for their romantic activity and while their hearts may be in the love scenes, they won't be in the play. It is a distraction that the other people involved in the play don't need. Besides, there will be enough problems resulting from romances originating in amateur theatre activity—late night rehearsal activity, constant proximity, intimate love scenes, etcetera—without starting out with such a problem when casting.

Still another thing to keep in mind when casting is the rehearsal schedule. It may be cruel, but the woman with small children and no household help is a bad choice for a cast which may have to have frequent late-night rehearsals. Likewise the man who has to get up especially early to go to work. An essential part of casting the play is making those who are trying out for the parts aware of what will be expected from them in the way of rehearsals. Resolve the time problems of individuals when you're casting them. The best actress in the world will be of no use to you if she can't get to rehearsals.

The same sort of reasoning applies when it comes to an actor's ability to project. The most sensitive of thespians is useless if he or she can't be heard by the audience. As director, you should be aware of the acoustical limits of the hall in which your group is performing. A performance which may seem sensitive in a small audition room may be lost on a stage in a large auditorium. Before the final selection of your cast, you should test them on the stage where they will perform. You should sit at the rear-most point in the house and make sure that a whispered line can be heard. This is not a matter of loudness. It is a matter of projection. It is very difficult to teach. To save yourself future headaches, make it a major consideration when you are casting.

One last word about casting may seem to conflict with what was said before about the advantages of casting an actor who looks the part. It has to do with using unusual casting to achieve some special or unusual effect in the play. Not all plays lend themselves to this sort of casting, but a few recent ones do. Among these is Kurt Vonnegut's *Happy Birthday Wanda June*.

The title role is actually a minor part in the play. Wanda June is a child who has been run over by an ice-cream truck and her speeches are delivered from a portion of the stage raised to indicate Heaven. Her lines are black humor and their effect stems from the childish naivete with which they are delivered.

In a production of the play by the Hollis Unitarian Drama Group in Queens, New York, Wanda June was played by an adult woman dressed in a child's party dress with sparkles on her costume and in her hair. She spoke in a high, piping falsetto. Although, removed from the context of the play, this may sound like a rather forced pprtrayal, in actuality it proved much more effective than if a child had played the part. All of the characters in "Heaven" picked up on the exaggeration and the result was a hilarious contrast between them and the "live" characters in the mainline of the play.

Quite incidentally—because it was irrelevant to both the portrayal and the play itself—the actress who portrayed Wanda June was a black woman. Due to the consciousness raising of the times in which we live, many amateur drama groups are making a threefold discovery concerning the casting of their black members. Every amateur director should be aware of the three possibilities.

First, there is the opportunity to cast blacks in roles that are more usually associated with whites. Indeed, the part may have been written for a white actor or actress. The part of Othello, after all, was written by Shakespeare with only white actors in mind. (It wasn't until the early 1930s that Paul Robeson became the first black man in the Twentieth Century to play the title role in a professional American production of *Othello*.) In the vast majority of roles in most plays, a portrayal by a black actor or actress will

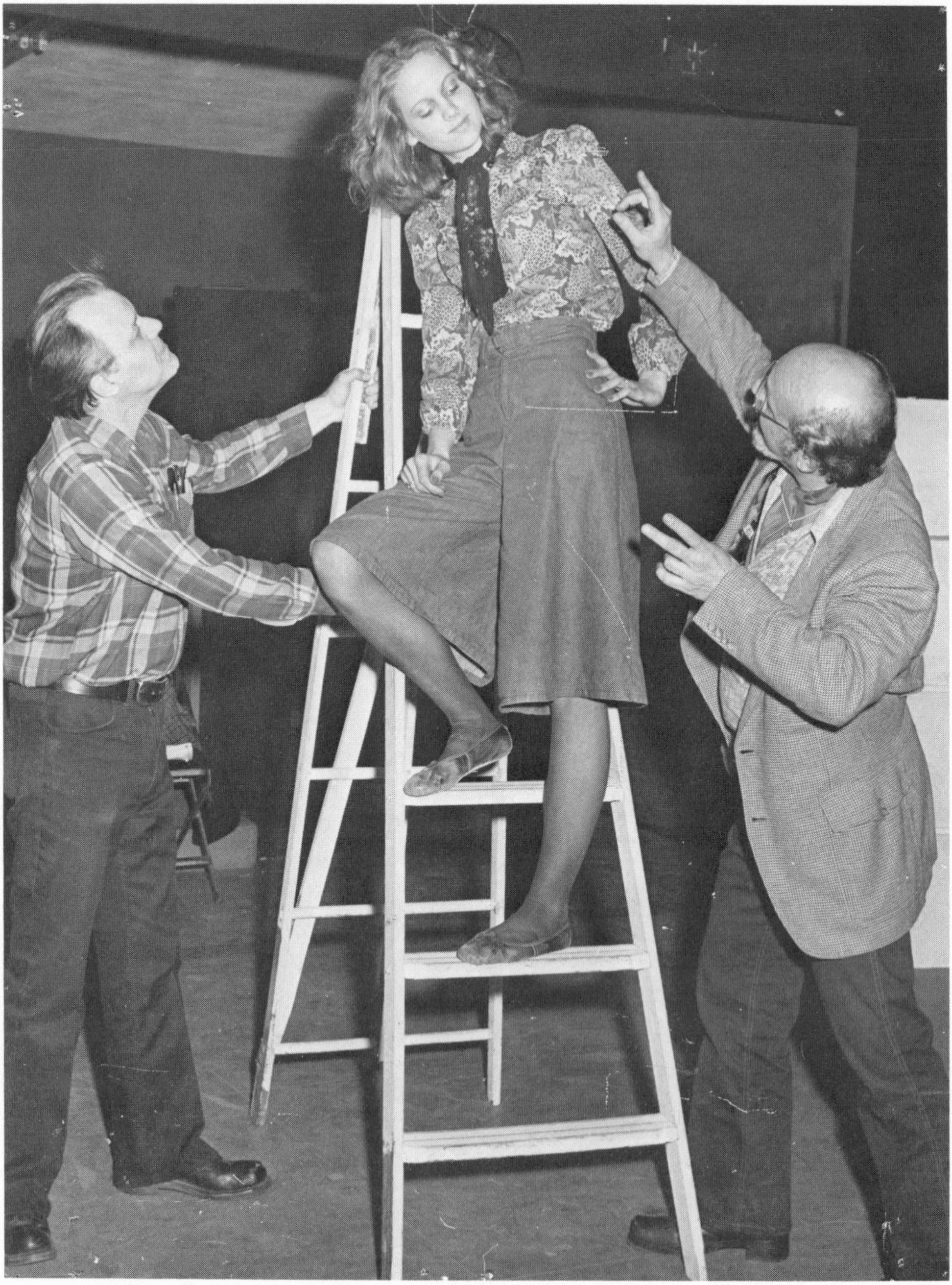

The director demonstrates the pose he wishes the actress to strike in a community theatre rehearsal of the highly stylized *Six Characters in Search of an Author.*

make little or no difference to the context of the plot. For instance, any one of the characters—minor or major—in Genet's *The Balcony* could be portrayed by a black performer without noticeably altering the meaning of the script. Likewise, almost any of the zanies (including the lead) in *The Man Who Came to Dinner* could as easily be black as white. And in most of today's romantic comedies, given our changing times, one or both of the lovers could be played by a black person. Indeed, some traditionally "white" plays—*Anna Lucasta* and *Guys and Dolls* come to mind—have been entirely cast with black performers and been very successful. In most cases involving amateur productions, where the group has a mixture of black and caucasian, talent is far more relevant to casting than skin color. The audience may be initially jarred by seeing a black person in a part that in their mind is associated with a white performer, but after five minutes this will be forgotten and the play will once again become the thing.

Second, there are certain plays—the best-written ones usually—which are open to a variety of interpretations and a variety of depths in the way their characters are played. A director who casts a black actor in such a part may discover a wealth of hidden meaning in the play. As an example, the Long Island Studio Theatre put on Edward Albee's *The Zoo Story* with an extremely talented black actor playing the part of Peter, the "over-civilized" park bench sitter who is bullied by the existential hippie, Jerry. Performed at a time when black-white confrontations were making headlines, the sensitive portrayal of Peter provided nuances to the play which were both beyond Albee's original script and yet well within the context of that human behavior with which the Albee play concerns itself.

Third, there are parts which are written explicitly for blacks, just as there are many recent plays written by blacks which have collectively gained respect as black theatre. One such part is the young black subway rider in LeRoi Jones' powerful drama *Dutchman*. Another is the part of the lover in Bruce Jay Friedman's *Scuba Duba*. And still another is the part of the killer in *Slow Dance on the Killing Ground*. If your group is not an all-black group, but has talented blacks in it, you should strongly consider doing plays with roles written specifically for blacks. Such consideration will greatly widen the range of plays available for your group to perform. As a director, such plays will also widen your directorial scope and enable you to maximally utilize the talents in your group.

A director may well have the most creative opportunity of anybody involved in the production of a play. The very first chance he has to exercise this creativity is when he is casting. We have discussed the creative vista opened up by casting a black man as Peter in *The Zoo Story*. Another amateur director we know has an even more imaginative idea involving this modern classic. He wants to cast two women as the play's protagonists. He wants to see what happens to Albee's abrasive dialogue when it is delivered by females. He is sure there are hidden meanings in the play which will emerge under the benefit of this casting.

Perhaps he is right. Perhaps he is wrong. Perhaps an audition by women will give him the answer. Perhaps a first serious reading. No matter. He is casting creatively, and that is the first step to directing creatively.

When casting has been completed, the director calls the entire cast together, and sitting around a table, or surrounding him in a circle, they read the play. Some great directors, Jed Harris in particular, continue this quiet reading of the play for several rehearsal periods. Throughout these first meetings, the director makes suggestions about characterization, explores motivations, points out hidden or subtle meanings, and makes corrections in line readings. This makes everyone familiar with all the people of the play, their reactions to one another, their kinships, liaisons, hostilities, phobias, affections, and so on. Correcting line readings, however, is anathema to many. Delving into the whys and wherefores of the thought behind each line takes time and bores the actors, while a quick correct reading by the director may immediately shed light on the meaning intended by the playwright. The actor then repeats the line as the director indicates, and no time is lost. Still, some directors revel in long discussions about motivations and meanings. The same end eventually is reached, so no harm is done by a director of this ilk, since time is not of the essence in most community theatres. Nevertheless, it seems to me that it should be remembered that a rehearsal room is not a schoolroom.

Once the cast is well aware of the play and its characters through the readings and discussions, the director starts to position the actors, which is known as "blocking." This again involves the stage manager. He will have marked out the floor of the rehearsal space with colored tape, showing the confines of the playing area as it will be when the scenery is in place. The tape will show the various openings, where doors or arches will be, so that the entrances and exits of the actors can be marked from the beginning. There should be chairs, tables, and benches in their proper places, and the director should have them used as is called for by the action. If possible, hand props also should be furnished, although using them early in rehearsals may be too much for some players. It is often too much for professionals.

There was the famous case of a film star returning to the theatre where she had really had very little experience prior to her Hollywood career. During rehearsal she burst into tears because she couldn't "get the hang," as she put it, of "walking on a line" (crossing the stage while speaking a line), carrying a book to be placed on a far table, and taking a puff of a cigarette on the way. Fortunately, she had a patient director who worked with her tirelessly, to the considerable consternation of the rest of the company. But in the end it paid off. The play was a hit, and so was the star. And her handling of the props was impeccable.

"Props," as I imagine everyone knows, is a contraction of "properties," which is a word covering everything moveable on a stage. All props are in the charge of the property man. In the Broadway theatre, the union allows no one but the property man, or men, to so much as touch a prop. I once casually rearranged some stage flowers which looked too stiff and artificial for my taste, and I was gently but firmly reprimanded by my own property man.

Before any of the final blocking and handling of props begins, the director must have done his homework and know how far into the play he will go on the first day, and also know more or less exactly where in the script and on what lines and to which positions he will direct the actors to walk, or sit or stand. This preliminary blocking is necessary to the director's concept of the play even if he only does it in his own head. It can be accomplished by the director taking his script to the empty stage and pacing off his first ideas of the action as he reads through it. The notes he makes in the margin at this point will be changed many times before the blocking is finalized. Nevertheless, they will be a basis from which he can proceed. Later, during one of the first rehearsals, he can have his cast walk through their lines while he moves them around and tests out different positions and crossings, etcetera. Being able to see the people move around will give him a visual basis for correcting his blocking.

Also, memorizing the lines will be easier for the actors if they associate them with certain movements they are making, or certain positions they are taking. Having a script at home and trying to memorize it before rehearsals start is difficult, even for the trained professional. But it is important that everyone have a pretty good idea of the "sense" of the lines their characters will speak, and a firm feeling of the character. After rehearsals start, reading and re-reading the lines, which have been marked off in the scripts with a colored pencil, is helpful.

When I started in the theatre, the actors were given only "sides" (their own lines) and the cue for the lines, which often was only the last three or four words spoken by another actor. They did not know what the play was about, or what the other characters were saying until rehearsals began. Sometimes directors expected the cast to be pretty familiar with their lines on the first day.

I never could understand this method. As soon as I was in the executive end of production, I asked to have the actors all given the entire play before rehearsals. "Too expensive," I was told. So I sat up all night typing copies of the script for everyone. That was way back when I was casting director and girl-of-all-work for famous Broadway producer, John Golden. A fascinating job, it was the foundation for all the work I have done in the theatre since then.

Some stage managers, including Herman Shapiro, who was my stage manager at City Center for years and years, make a large diagram of the floor of the set, marking it off with numbers, starting with number one at the main entrance to the set and continuing the numbers around the set and furniture. Then instead of writing "Father goes stage left to left end of sofa," he merely writes the position number to be followed, so that moves can be marked at specific words or directions in the script. It is much quicker and more easily understood for the stage manager to write "F74 to 69, sits" than the longer version.

However, in most of the plays which community theatres produce, the moves are already marked in what are called "stage managers' acting versions," which means that all the work done by the original director and stage manager has been noted and printed and can be more or less easily followed by other directors. But in managers' acting versions," which means that all the work done by from a proscenium setting to a thrust stage, or "in-the-round," or because of a whole new conception on the part of the director, a different set of movements may be desirable. Then it is important that the stage manager keep a clear record of them.

There is a strong feeling among many amateur directors that these "stage managers' acting versions" have the potential to do more harm than good when they fall into the hands of the actors.

These directors feel that all blocking should grow out of their concept of the play and that every director's concept will be different. This difference will stem not just from the limitations of the playing area, but also from the basic way in which he approaches the play. Given these two factors, the directions for movement which appear in these versions are almost never valid. They throw the actors off and frequently they create conflicts between the actor and the director. In such conflicts the actor invariably cites the stage manager's script as the authority and the poor director, his own authority undercut, must spend precious rehearsal time explaining why he has found it necessary to alter the actions. Directors who feel this way sometimes go over these scripts with a magic marker before giving them to the actors and cross out all stage directions in such a way that they cannot be read. (The same thinking applies to directions for movements, gestures, smiles and emotions, and some directors also black these out.)

In general, when blocking a play for amateur production, the less you move your actors around, the better. This is particularly true when there are more than two actors on stage at one time. One actor crossing the stage at the wrong time, or in the wrong place, can precipitate a traffic jam which may throw off the timing for the entire scene and "lose" the audience. When there are many people on the stage at one time, moving them around even when the show is not a musical involves a sort of choreography. A good example of this problem was an amateur production of *Spoon River Anthology*—a production which was more of a dramatic recital with music than an outright musical. There were thirty people on stage at the same time and constant crossovers involving many or all of them. The action had to be timed and executed perfectly so that one sequence would blend into the next without distraction. But there was one problem performer who simply could not remember where to move during these shifts. He kept getting his directions confused and when, during rehearsals, he ended up in the wrong spot, he would compound his error by delivering—out of sequence—the speech he associated with the place where he had come to rest. The result was that he not only threw himself off, but everybody else as well. The director tried everything, but the fellow had a block and was quite simply unable to remember his movements correctly. Finally, out of desperation, the director devised a rather drastic solution. He had the other actors memorize where the problem actor was supposed to move, and whenever he started out in the wrong direction, one of them would stick out a foot and trip him. By the time the play actually went before an audience, this ploy was working well enough so that it was enough to simply block the actor with a leg when he started to move in the wrong direction without actually tripping him. Thus the audience was slightly puzzled by the actors' needs to so frequently stretch their legs, but spared the sight of the guilty party sprawling over the stage. Typically, it was the problem actor who received a majority of the opening night kudos for his "poise" on stage—as contrasted with the nervousness of other actors who had not only to worry about themselves, but him as well.

If groups of people on stage present blocking problems, the director should also be cognizant of how to achieve the effect he desires with only one or two people. In a monologue, for instance, positioning the actor at the rear of the stage will create an effect of psychological as well as physical depth and lend his words authority and perhaps portentousness. Positioning him at stage-front, even on the lip of the stage, will create an intimacy with the audience. In the Broadway production of Albee's Pulitzer Prize winning play *A Delicate Balance*, Tobias' long monologue about his cat was delivered by Hume Cronyn from fairly far to the rear of the stage so as not to destroy the "coldness" of the character he was playing, an emotion which was integral to the plot of the play. Just about every amateur production emulates this staging although the director may never have seen the professional show. The reason is that instinct dictates the need for the distance from the audience. It is a high point of the show, and the one community theatre production I saw which performed the show in the round fell flat with the cat monologue because Tobias was too close to his audience for the speech to create the mood of cold menace necessary to the action which follows.

Conversely, in *The Iceman Cometh*, the 45-minute monologue was delivered by Jason Robards right to the audience from various positions at front and center stage. The character is taking the audience into his confidence, enlisting their support for his point of view. The charisma of an actor like Robards works wonders in this scene. But less charismatic actors in community theatre have to fall back on the techniques of staging, and it is up to the director to see to it that they are used to best advantage. The time to start thinking about this is when the director is first considering the blocking.

With two people on a stage in a dramatic scene, for instance, the first thing the director has to consider is just exactly what effect he is trying to achieve. Does he want conflict? Then his actors

Many community theatre directors are finding the results rewarding when they cast black actors in roles not explicitly written for them. On the other hand, in some cases, as with Bruce Jay Friedman's *Scuba Duba* (above), the play itself dictates such casting. *(Picture courtesy of Long Island Studio Theatre, Lindenhurst, N.Y.)* The director must always be aware of the pacing and allow for laughs in comedies like *Scapino* (below). *(Picture courtesy Mariemont Players, Inc., Cincinnati, Ohio.)*

should be positioned at opposite ends of the stage with the playing area between them transformed into a battleground which should crackle with the dialogue. Intimacy? Then they should be close together and towards the front of the stage, although not necessarily the center. Does he want one actor to dominate? Then the other actor should be positioned downstage from him. Throughout the early meetings the director should be planning out these moves and conveying them to actors during those early line rehearsals which may not take place on the actual stage.

Once the actors know where to go on the set and how to use their hand props—which, by the way, keeps them too busy to become self-conscious—the director should break the acts into scenes for them. He will rehearse them in the opening scene, usually called "the establishing scene," which may be between two people and run only a few pages. When another character enters, a second scene begins. A play is composed of a series of these scenes, and the published versions of some old plays—especially those in French—helpfully number each scene. Modern plays, as we know, are written in acts, two or three of them, as a rule, and leave it up to the director to outline the scenes. Each scene has a unity of its own and an expert director builds these scenes carefully, giving each one a beginning and an end, then blends one scene into another until the act comes to its finish. It is most unwise for a director to let his players ramble on without regard for these beginnings and ends of scenes. The result is rather like trying to read a page of sentences without punctuation. Director Gene Saks, a master of defining scenes in comedies, gives the impression of proceeding at top speed while actually the pace is rather deliberate. Other directors try to emulate him, urge the actors to speak and move faster and faster, and achieve only a frantic racing about, with great loss of comedy values. Still, as will be discussed, fast pacing, done properly, is important to a play.

As the director and stage manager continue their work, they must both keep the actors aware of various effects, such as light changes, and various sounds. Light changes can be indicated by the stage manager softly saying, "The sun is beginning to set," or "Lights come full up," or whatever. Sounds, too, should be used from the start of rehearsals. A handbell can be used by the stage manager to simulate the ringing of a telephone or doorbell, or he can merely say, "Telephone," or "Doorbell." He can stamp his foot for a door slam or off-stage crash, and call out "dog barks," if needed. Or maybe the stage manager will try his talent at an "arff-

arff" for the dog and break up the company. The director should not be annoyed at this. The more relaxed and amused he can keep his company (without losing discipline), the better his results will be. He also should stay sympathetic to difficulties the actors encounter in memorizing the lines, maintaining their concentration and energy, floundering in their movements and even forgetting them. He must be all-understanding and helpful and try his best not to become irritable.

Admittedly it is pretty difficult to remain on an even keel when the leading lady not only cannot remember her lines, but skips rehearsals and is late to those she does attend. But when the director discovers that her husband is out of work, she is holding down a demanding job, and has four children, three dogs, two cats and a canary to look after and feed, he can be tolerant. That is, if he knows her heart is in the work and in the end she will play her part well.

I am told by some directors that discipline is difficult to maintain in community theatre work. Other directors say that if they start out by making it clearly understood that everyone is expected to help the director and help themselves by doing their best in the way of attending rehearsals, being on time for them, keeping quiet when not in scenes being rehearsed, etc., and all agree, the sailing is comparatively smooth. Anyone coming late after that, they say, comes in a state of embarrassment and apology and does not let it happen again.

Children in the cast pose an extra difficulty for the director. Usually they are the offspring of members of the company. If the parent is not also in the play, however, it is important that the director insist that the parent be present at all times the child is at rehearsals. Children respond well to direction if they have any real desire to be in a play, and if they do not, they should not be considered, nepotism notwithstanding.

As a rule, acting is a game to children and they enjoy being the center of attention during their scenes. These should be scheduled early and gotten over with so they may leave promptly. When they are not at work, the parent is responsible for keeping them quiet and out of the way. I am speaking of small children. Those ten years and older are pretty sophisticated these days and can take care of themselves nicely.

One fourteen-year-old, who started as an actor with the New Milford Community Theatre, is now their favorite "lighting expert." He has always been a dedicated worker and once during a blizzard he was shocked when no one showed up for a rehearsal he didn't realize had been cancelled. "A little snow wouldn't have killed them," he grumbled to the caretaker who had opened the door for him. "I'll just stay and do my work without them." When he was twelve he was an assistant stage manager and wanted to quit in the middle of a rehearsal which was not going well. The director asked why. "Because," the youngster answered, "everything in the theatre should be perfect and I don't think I am." "No one and nothing in the theatre is perfect," the director screamed. "Go back and get to work!" That's a good thing to remember when things go wrong.

When the director encounters a scene which proves difficult for the actors and in which the pace is halting and the rhythm broken, usually because one of the actors if floundering, it is best to go over the scene repeatedly until the process of memory becomes automatic for everyone, in both lines and action, and the scene runs smoothly. The actor who is at fault cannot do it alone. He needs the momentum created by all the actors in the scene to bolster him up and carry him along until all is well.

There are many techniques for this sort of line reading. One which is most efficacious is to have the cast sitting around in a circle delivering their lines in an absolute monotone, deliberately divorced from all meaning which the words may have been meant to convey. The idea is to reduce the cues to sounds triggering mechanical responses which in turn will trigger other mechanical responses. The actors usually hate this (it is boring!) but some directors swear by it as a means of solving memorization problems.

Directors also like it for another reason. It is a way of getting the actors to pick up the pace and rhythm of the play. By the time the scene is being gone over a third or fourth time, the cues will not only be picked up much more quickly, but the lines themselves will be delivered with more speed. Almost without exception, a play is improved by picking up the pace.

Amateur actors are not very good judges of the pace and rhythm of their own delivery. Ultimately the audience will judge them, of course, but by that time it will be too late to correct mistakes. Thus it is the director's job to determine the pace and rhythm and to see that his actors maintain both.

An inexperienced actor's natural inclination is to deliver each of his lines to the audience as if it had been carved in stone by the playwright. He wants to extract every last drop of meaning from

The director has to judge the length of time an emotion can be sustained. One example of how delicate this judgment must be is the death scene from *Tiny Alice* (above). *(Picture courtesy of Long Island Studio Theatre of Lindenhurst, N.Y.)* The most delicate balance of *A Delicate Balance* (below) is positioning six active actors on stage at the same time. Most community theatres have playing areas much smaller than the one shown here. *(Picture courtesy of Midland Community Theatre, Inc., Midland, Texas.)*

the words. If all of these actors had their way, a normal two hour drama could last through the night.

The director must know which are the throwaway lines—and this means more of the dialogue than you might think in most plays—and set a pace that will keep his actors from lingering over them. Back-and-forth comedy banter should be rapid (with pauses for laughs during the actual production, of course) and the director should see to it that the actors work out a rhythm in which they "bounce" their lines off each other. The same applies to a dramatic scene. A rhythm should come out of the material itself, and if it doesn't come naturally, the director should help the actors to extract it. And once the rhythm has been established, the pace should almost always be speeded up.

Plays are largely made up of words with actions calculated to make the words more effective. And yet one of the most frequent negative critical judgments leveled against a play is that it is "too wordy." This is also a common complaint of audiences at amateur productions. Sometimes "too wordy" means just what it says, and the fault lies with the playwright. But much more often it really is a reaction to lack of verbal rhythm between actors and turgid pacing. Always this is the director's responsibility to correct. The amateur director's most frequent comment should be "Pick up the pace!"

Another difficulty some directors encounter is with exit lines. They should always be spoken at or near the exit, especially if the line is laugh-provoking, or an applause rouser. It makes for bad timing, and ruins the pace of the show if the actor is center-stage, reads the line, gets the laugh or applause, and *then* walks to the exit. If he moves at once upon speaking the line, he will kill the laugh or applause and if he waits he will have to walk on another actor's line, or what is worse, on "dead air." I have seen this happen more than once, but not on Broadway.

An equally threatening occurrence, from the director's point of view, is the establishment of a laugh reflex in an actor or actress. This is, naturally, most likely to occur if you're doing a comedy. What happens is that one actor's delivery of a line is so hilarious that it evokes genuine laughter from one or more members of the cast. Or it may even set off the speaker himself.

The first time this happens, the wise director will simply let it pass. He or she may even join in the hilarity. The first time is not a threat. It is when it occurs again at exactly the same point in the script that it becomes dangerous. A third time involving the same actor or actors, and you've got a problem on your hands. Pretty soon the actor who delivers the line begins building a nervous apprehension which either prevents him from delivering the line at all, causes him to garble it, or prods him to deliver it with an explosive giggle. The other actors are also anticipating a laugh, perhaps fighting against it in ways which are throwing off their timing or cues, and are therefore to some extent not "in the play."

This syndrome does not occur only in comedy. It sometimes happens in melodrama that a really heart-rending line will trigger a defensive giggle instead of a tear. Again, if it becomes habit, it will become very destructive of the performance given before an audience.

What can be done to prevent it? The director can insist to the actor that he concentrate on controlling himself and suggest to the company that they help him do so. This should carry the actor past the line which starts him laughing.

Incidentally, a distinction should be made between this problem and the fact that if a good laugh line is delivered on stage all of the actors should react to it within the context of the play. To laugh when something is funny is normal, and such a reaction is acceptable as long as it doesn't get out of hand. Indeed, normal reactions are the key to an actor's staying "in the play."

No one on a stage is "out of the play," even if he does not speak for some time. A director should never let anyone stand around absentmindedly thinking about what he will have for supper, or how the baby is, when another actor has a long speech or other actors are playing a scene. The presence and mental attitude of everyone in view are always felt by an audience.

It is the director's duty to stress this from the very first time his actors rehearse on a stage. Community theatre is a fun activity, and sometimes it is not very much fun to sit like a bump on a log while another actor delivers his or her lines. But if the director lets the non-speaking actor indulge his propensity to direct his attention elsewhere in the early rehearsals, as with the laugh-reflex, habit will be created, a habit of inattention which will really hurt the play when it is being done for an audience.

"But how can I be interested in a line I've heard delivered fifty times?" the actor may wail.

The answer is that he can't be, but the other part of the answer is that he is supposed to be *acting*. If he can't force himself to really listen, then he must *act* as though he were listening.

One thing he can try is picking up a prop and focusing on that and playing with it to keep himself "in the play." Film performances are not usually germane to community theatre, but one which does demonstrate this particular point is Marlon Brando's acclaimed performance in *On The Waterfront*. Here, in a scene with Eva Marie Saint, as an inarticulate longshoreman he took her glove in his hands and played with it all through the scene. It was such an effective ploy that buffs of film acting still point it out as a prime example of an actor developing his character while his co-star does almost all of the talking. Only Brando knows if it was true in his case, but as a general rule for community theatre directors instructing actors and actresses, this is a worthwhile ploy to remember in overcoming the bad habit of inattention on stage. Always remember, however, that the director should make clear that if this is not done very subtly, it will become a distraction to the main action and make worse the very problem it is trying to cure.

Another bad habit many community theatre players—and some professionals—have is that of heralding a laugh line by an exaggerated and audible gulping of air before reading the line. This used to be prevalent and very annoying among character comediennes on Broadway, but close-up work in films and television has made it such an apparent nuisance that they gradually have abandoned it.

Once all of these—and other—difficulties are out of the way, and all the scenes have been defined and blended into the acts, "run-throughs" should start. After a week of them, the director and actors might invite a few friends to come in to rehearsals in order to give the cast an idea of audience reaction. This is most helpful for timing, especially for a comedy. An audience of only fifteen or twenty people, not allowed to spread out, but placed close together, can give a pretty good idea of what will happen on opening night. If the director and all those connected with the production find they cannot gather together that many visitors, they can postpone this exposure and wait until dress rehearsal, when it is absolutely essential to have an audience.

Several dress rehearsals are ideal, even a week of them. In the professional theatre, when a play is not taken out of town for a tryout (in order to avoid that considerable expense), it is given numerous "preview" performances so that the cast can benefit by just that necessary audience reaction before facing the critics on opening night. If this is true on Broadway, how much more necessary it is in community theatre.

chapter 5

Acting

I ALREADY HAVE mentioned that Shakespeare is difficult for American actors because they do not or cannot "speak the lines trippingly on the tongue." This is true, however, not only in speaking Shakespeare's immortal words, but often in general. American actors' speech is sloppy. They swallow the ends of their lines. They do not know how to project their voices properly, and often they shout in order to be heard in a large theatre. If this is true of the trained actor, how can amateurs be expected to do better? Oddly enough, in many cases I have found that they do. Perhaps because their theatres have been smaller or the acoustics better, I have been able to hear the players satisfactorily. Often I have been impressed by the clarity of their diction.

While, as previously stated, the finest performance is valueless if it cannot clearly be heard, its impact also is lessened if the actor, either professional or amateur, resorts to an exaggerated preciseness, or "elocution." When the manner of speaking the playwright's words distracts the audience from the meaning of them, all is lost.

It seems to me that fine acting, or lecturing, teaching, or preaching, for that matter, is the ability to transfer the thought behind the words to the listeners as directly and as clearly as possible. It is thrilling to me to see how an actor can dominate an audience. This is truly the star quality one hears so much about, the presence felt when a powerful personality speaks.

This star quality is said to be something one is born with, but I believe it also can be developed. Certainly the ability to transfer thoughts can be learned. It has to do with the actor's concentration, and his awareness of his audience, and its concentration on him as the character he is portraying, and what that character is saying. This is a gift the born public speaker in any category has, but everyone trying to be a skillful actor should learn it. It just takes time and hard work.

It may be true that actors in community theatre are not as hard-working or as committed to their jobs as professionals. They usually are acting for the sheer fun of it, but still they can give effective and heart-warming performances. What they lack in experience and technique, they can make up for with an inner belief and an uninhibited exuberance. Aided by a perceptive director who can edit a performance which might otherwise go overboard, they can bring a character to life with unusual clarity and humor and sometimes stimulate an audience to bravos.

Of course, there are many members of community theatres who look at it simply as an added social activity. They like the camaraderie of the group and the fun of playing another person, especially when that character is an amusing one, with nice built-in laugh-lines. Others find it a necessary source of self-expression and still others revel in it as a life-long avocation. No matter the reason. A fine performance is possible for everyone.

Sometimes, after seeing one of these particularly fine amateur performances, I go backstage to meet the actor who has impressed me and I ask him the obvious: "Have you ever been a professional actor?" Usually the answer is no—with an explanation. He did have successful experiences in high school or college, and he did intend to go to New York and try to join the ranks of the professional actor, but instead he married and pursued a steady income. Or his father needed him in the family business. Or his friends talked him out of it. Anyway, at present he says he is well satisfied to be part of the community theatre where he has become a favorite and his ego is more than satisfied. Also, the publicity he receives is good for his business and his social life. And his family likes it all, too.

When I ask another actor, "Wouldn't you like to try your luck in the professional theatre?" the answer is an emphatic "No!" But sometimes there is a wistful word or so following which gives me the impression that it really has been his life's desire, but he's just never worked up the courage to take the plunge. Often it is, I am told, the fear of rejection. Sometimes it seems to be the more basic fear of being unable to make a living.

In the case of one former amateur who did take the plunge, he answered "yes" to that second question after more than twenty years in community theatre work. Ulu Grosbard, the director, was having a difficult time finding the right actor for a role in his off-Broadway production of Arthur Miller's *A View from the Bridge* when he was told of this amateur actor who "looked the part" and had a reputation of giving consistently good performances with his theatre group. Ulu went to see Jack Somack at work, was impressed and offered him the part. Jack was thrilled. He had had a successful career as an electrical engineer, did not have to worry about making a living, and he accepted Ulu's invitation with delight.

Shortly after this we were casting *The Country Girl* for our revival at City Center, and I needed a strong, prepossessing actor for the part of Phil Cook, the producer. This was a short but vital role, difficult to cast because it was not considered important enough for well-known or established actors. Someone told me about Jack's performance in the Arthur Miller play and it was not long before I had seen his excellent work and arranged with Ulu to give Jack a two weeks' leave of absence. (We scheduled our plays for only two or three week runs because our 3,000 seat house enabled forty to sixty thousand theatregoers to attend our performances in that time!) That was Jack's introduction to Broadway, and he has been working professionally ever since, sometimes making close to a hundred thousand dollars a year (but mostly from television work and commercials, I hate to admit). He is the actor, by the way, who made famous that "Mama mia, that's-a mighty spicy meatball" commercial for Alka Seltzer. But Jack always says it was community theatre work which gave him the background, training and self-confidence that made it all possible.

Not all community theatre actors are that gifted. But their love of acting gives them a special quality, and with some experience, their shortcomings seem insignificant. Experience, as a matter of fact, is a better teacher in community theatre than are most directors who often are untrained.

These directors too often settle for the physical movement or placing of the players, and they are not always skillful enough at that. However, if an actor finds he has been placed where he is partially hidden from the audience by a piece of furniture or by another player, he can quickly make his own adjustment. It is wiser for him to do so without comment. At first the director may protest, but usually he soon sees the improvement that has been made by the actor's few steps. Sometimes even "up-staging" is overlooked. "Up-staging" is when one actor positions himself in back of another actor to whom he is speaking, which makes that poor fellow turn his back and face away from the audience during the conversation. This used to be a favorite maneuver of old-fashioned stars intent on being the center of attention. In community theatre it is usually not purposely done, but is just an error in blocking which should be corrected for everyone's sake, particularly the audience.

However, if the same scene is redirected, so that the two actors are standing face to face, their bodies, faces and feet lateral to the audience, there is not that much improvement. It will look better and the audience will hear the lines better if the scene is played eye-to-eye, but with both faces turned slightly toward the front of the stage, and the downstage feet of both actors slightly back and pointed toward the front, rather than strictly lateral and together. This makes a more graceful picture than a nose-to-nose confrontation, unless that is done to make a comedy point. Also, more of the actors' expressions can be seen and their voices will not shoot off into the wings.

When more than two actors are on stage, but not all are included in the scene being played, it is important that they nevertheless "stay in the scene," listening to what is being said, but not reacting in any way to detract form what is going on, unless the director wishes otherwise. Every actor on stage is part of a pattern, and should always remain in character, whether speaking lines in that scene or not. Helen Hayes once said, "Being part of a scene but not speaking in that scene poses a problem for the best actor."

One technique for doing this, as was shown in the chapter on directing, is to relate to a prop. But while that is a technique a director may recommend to an actor, it is not really an answer to the problem of mutely "staying in the scene" unless the actor himself finds it valid. The director can identify the problem and recommend solutions, but it is up to the individual actor to devise a method which will work for himself.

One amateur actor who played Peter in *The Zoo Story* and had to sit still and listen silently to Jerry's twenty-minute monologue during rehearsal after rehearsal solved the problem of "staying in the scene" by a ploy which every playwright must applaud. He concentrated intensely on the words to which he was listening and sought new meanings in them each night, meanings which would add understanding and depth to his response when he finally made it. The fact that his initial reply to the monologue is "I don't understand" might seem at odds to this approach. In fact, his listening made him change his delivery of those three words twice. He

The ultimate aim of actors is to gain the audience's involvement. This was done by the players in *Marat/Sade* (above) by physically carrying the play up the aisles through the audience. In *Who's Afraid of Virginia Woolf?* (below) the involvement was captured by the intensity of the actress' portrayal. *(Pictures courtesy of Long Island Studio Theatre of Lindenhurst, N.Y.)*

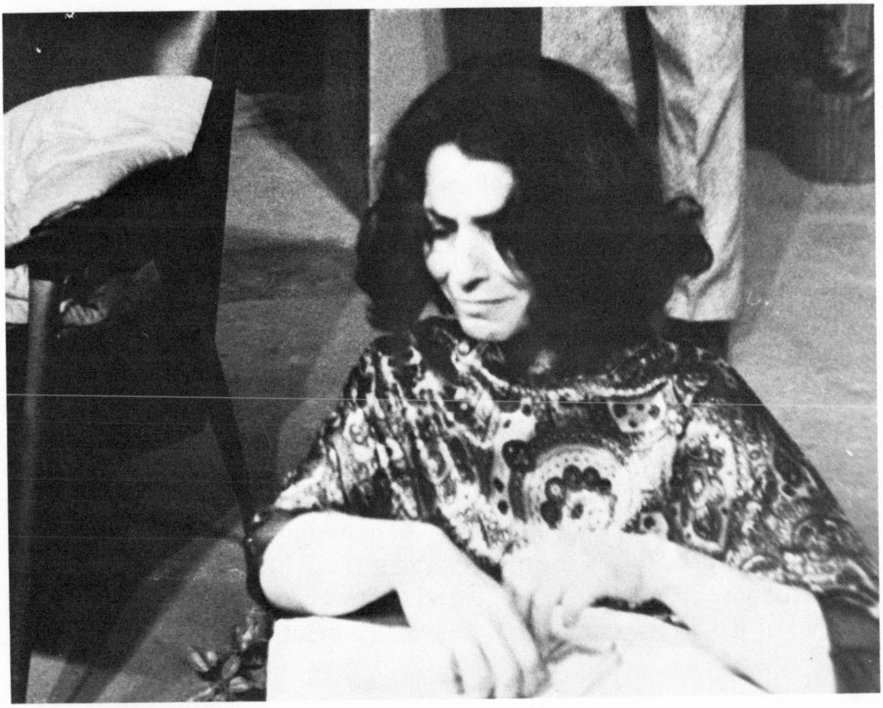

started out delivering them literally. (Jerry had told him a distasteful, but seemingly irrelevant story about poisoning a dog, and it seemed that Peter really would not understand.) Then, after listening intently, he decided that when Peter says "I don't understand," he really does understand but is so discomfitted by Jerry's story that he must deny its meaning to him. Thus he delivered the line so that the audience should know he meant the opposite of what the words were saying. Finally, by searching the words for still more meaning while listening, he determined that they aroused in Peter a complex response in which he both does not understand the actual story Jerry is telling him, but understands all too well the emotion underlying the words. He is both threatened and attracted by the raw and arrogant plea for contact which is Jerry's monologue. When he says "I don't understand," all of this (the actor concluded) must be present. And he strove to use that line to propel him into the next scene with all of the different things Peter is feeling providing the drama for the action which follows.

Such a solution for "staying in the scene" approaches the ideal. Most amateur actors would not be capable of it. Truthfully, most monologues in most plays would not lend themselves to such concentration.

Still, the principle is sound. To really listen to the words being spoken is the actor's best guard against that inattention which is so readily communicated to the audience and which they so readily emulate. Training oneself to listen may well be the amateur actor's most valuable tool.

Another way of "staying in the scene" is by concentrating on the relationship the character you are playing has to the character delivering the monologue. This is a somewhat more detached method. It involves deciding in advance what your character feels towards the other character. Then it involves concentrating on that emotion and directing it towards the other character during the monologue.

Let us say the emotion is love. Prior to going onstage you should think about the character played by the actor to whom you will be listening. What is there about the character that really attracts you? Love itself is a strong emotion, but liking is a common one and usually easily accessible. Generally speaking, we can almost always find something we like about another person. Whatever it is, this is the quality about the character on which you must concentrate. Zero in on it and try to intensify your feeling for it until it will appear on stage as a representation of love.

The same principle applies to hate, or other emotions. The trick is to tie it in not with the whole person, but with some facet of the person which arouses the desired emotion. And then the trick is to concentrate on that facet during periods of enforced silence and inaction onstage.

In a larger context, Lee Strasberg says an actor's real problem is physical or muscular tension on stage. When there is tension in the body, one cannot think or feel adequately to do justice to the part being played. To overcome this, Lee suggests getting rid of tension before going on stage. His method for doing that is to relax while sitting in a chair, in such a comfortable position that it would be possible to go to sleep. Then one starts to tense or tighten the muscles, starting with the toes, then the feet, the ankles, calves of the legs and so on until the entire body is tense. After holding this tension for several seconds, sudden relaxation, letting the body go slack, brings freedom and comfort to the nervous system. If one time is not enough, the exercise can be repeated until all body tension is lost. Many of Lee's method actors would not think of going on stage without going through this exercise in the dressing room.

Other performers, both professional and amateur, develop their own techniques for relaxing before going onstage. Some find physical exercise, the more strenuous the better, helpful as a relaxation technique. One community theatre player with some twenty years experience behind him still does forty push-ups in the dressing room before every performance. Two others find physical competition helpful. They Indian handwrestle both before the performance and between the acts. An actress goes through a complex series of dance movements to put her at her ease before confronting the audience. And another actress skips rope in much the same manner as a prizefighter training for a match.

There are actors who massage each other before performances. There are those who take one or two drinks (but I don't recommend this; it throws the timing off). Some actors are into Transcendental Meditation and go off by themselves to recite their mantra before the play begins. Others use deep breathing, or yoga positions to clear their minds and relax their bodies. Still others read a book, or swap jokes with one another, or play cards, or checkers, or chess.

It isn't important which method—those mentioned here, or one of your own invention—you use to relax. What is important is that you do something to ease your tension. And whatever you do is valid just so long as it works for you.

When Walter Matthau, one of the most famous method actors, was just becoming recognized, he played with Helen Hayes in the City Center production of *The Wisteria Trees*, Joshua Logan's lovely version of Chekhov's *The Cherry Orchard*. Walter had many method exercises he liked to go through before going on stage. Before the scene with Helen where he was to come on after a long hard ride on horseback to announce that he has just bought her estate, Walter would jog in place until he was almost breathless, then dash on from stage right and exuberantly throw his hat in the air as he spoke his line. Helen and I both feared that his hat would sail out into the audience, and we thought it would be better if he came on hatless or threw his hat upstage with his left hand. However, he and the director thought that would not be natural, and, of course, on opening night Walter threw his hat right out into the audience, someone threw it back on stage, everybody thought that pretty funny, and the scene was ruined. We all forgave Walter, however, because his personal magnetism and intense concentration soon had the audience's attention back with him and Helen and they brought the play to a fine finish. Besides, we all loved Walter.

Nevertheless, body control is as important as spontaneity of emotion. The body is used for many dramatic or comedic effects. Good actors are good mimes and can play a lengthy scene without words, giving the audience complete satisfaction as to its meaning and significance through body language and facial expression. *Sleuth*, a two character play, has several long scenes with only one player on stage with no one to speak to, and he must continue the action and story line without words.

Body language is also used to enforce speech, on the stage as we use it in life. For example, banging a fist on the desk to emphasize "I forbid that!" or dropping limply into a chair to accompany "I am completely exhausted!"

Body language and facial expression are particularly important in playing comedy. Both the "larger than life" school and "the raised eyebrow" approach depend on the body and face as well as the voice to bring laughs. Over-acting and "mugging" (making extravagant facial expressions) are sometimes resorted to in community theatres and can have hilarious results. Since those performances are not being rated by the sensitive New York critics, no harm is done. But it is a habit that can go too far, and it should be monitored by the director.

In drama it is suicide to overplay. Dramatic moments can appear ludicrous and embarrassing if they are not strictly controlled. "Scene-chewing" is as dangerous in community theatre as it is on Broadway.

I once saw a production of Somerset Maugham's *Rain* with a famous singer playing the Reverend Davidson in a style better suited to the Metropolitan Opera House than to an intimate theatre. The result was that starting with politely suppressed giggles, the amusement of the audience grew so that finally every time the poor man spoke he was greeted by uncontrollable laughter.

The same thing happened to another unfortunate actor playing Anna's father, the old sea captain, in *Anna Christie*. It got so that every time he mentioned "Dat ol' dabbil sea," the audience broke up.

In amateur theatre there may be many causes of such unwanted laughter. One of the most common is the mishandled clinch scene. For whatever reasons of shyness and inhibition, the act of kissing is one of the most difficult actions for inexperienced actors to bring off convincingly on stage. And nothing is as risible to an audience as a kiss gone awry.

And why not? What could be funnier (and therefore perhaps more destructive of the desired mood) than two adults leaning towards each other like opposing tent poles (feet firmly dug into the stage) until their reluctant lips make gingerly contact. What could be more destructive of the portrayal of passion than mouths bouncing off each other like opposing magnetic particles? What could shatter intimacy for an audience so surely as bodies stiff as cadavers attempting an embrace?

Many a play, perhaps a majority, stands or falls on the successful portrayal of a love scene. Any two actors involved in such a scene in community theatre should be aware of its importance. (Some, it is true, are overly aware, and I have seen such couples destroy their love scenes by breaking into embarrassed giggles.) The efforts to overcome their inhibitions should begin with the very first rehearsals so that they are banished by the time the scene is being played in front of a paying audience.

It can of course be a sticky business in amateur groups where the two people involved in a love scene may be married to two other people entirely. Still, an adult approach must be taken if the play is to succeed. After all, on Broadway it is not unknown for actors who actively detest each other to play the most passionate love scenes convincingly.

One solution is for the two actors to go off alone together and try to frankly discuss with each other their inhibitions regarding the scene. It is important that neither see the other's reluctance to portray intimacy and love as a rejection. Such a perception will only increase the awkwardness of the situation.

Another solution is to discuss the scene alone with the director. If he is made aware of the problem from the beginning, then he can handle it in a helpful manner during rehearsals instead of perhaps inadvertently subjecting the pair to embarrassment by kidding co-actors. Also, he may be able to devise "exercises" for the actors to relieve the situation.

Some actors may prefer to work out their own exercises. These frequently take the form of what may seem silliness. But it is silliness with a purpose. Once two people—alone—have revealed themselves to each other by performing childish acts, they are much more likely to be relaxed with each other when it comes to embracing and kissing.

Such silliness may consist of the man, for instance, standing on one leg and singing "Yankee Doodle" slowly, dragging out each syllable distinctly, projecting at the top of his lungs. Or it may consist of the woman doing an improvisation of a hippopotamus bathing itself at a waterhole. Or the two of them may simply sit for twenty minutes or so, in silence, and make faces at each other.

The idea is to break the ice—and more. It is to get them to the point where they can physically display affection before an audience in a natural fashion. It will be up to the director to position them so that their love scene looks convincing to the audience, but no amount of positioning will be able to conceal how the actors really feel about each other. And how they really feel is what will be conveyed to those watching.

An example of this was a couple I saw doing a scene from *Detective Story* for a church-based community theatre performance. There came a point in the scene where the actor was supposed to lift the downcast face of the woman and kiss her. But when he cupped his hand gently under her chin, it proved immovable. He wedged his hand under her jaw and pushed harder. Still she resisted. The audience began to titter. He quickly gave up the attempt and went on to the next lines—which were considerably weakened without the kiss. Later, backstage, he asked his co-star why she had been so intractable.

"I never let anyone but my husband kiss me," she answered modestly.

"Now she tells me!" The actor went off railing at the heavens.

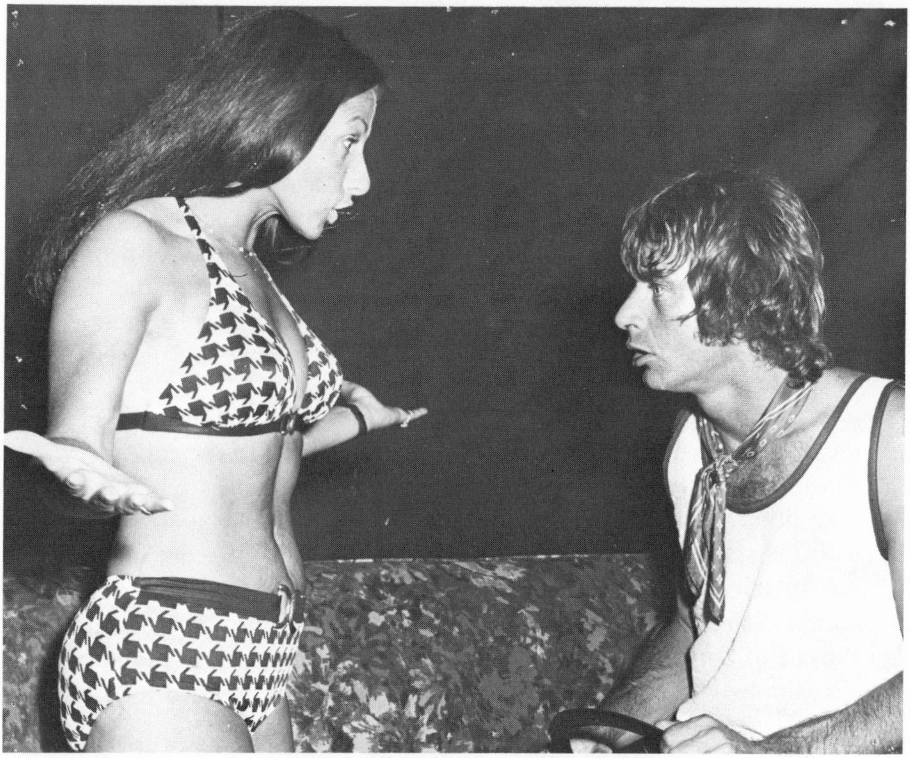

The easiest type of scene for actors to handle is between only two people, as in *Scuba Duba* (above) and *Sleuth* (below). *(Picture above courtesy Long Island Studio Theatre, Lindenhurst, N.Y. Picture below courtesy of Sunset Playhouse, Elm Grove, Wisc.)*

Of course this all should have been worked out in rehearsals. But when the actress had fudged the kiss during rehearsals, the actor had simply assumed that while she was shy about unnecessary intimacy, surely when the chips were down and there was an audience out there, she would indulge the osculation. A director would have perhaps insisted that they kiss during rehearsals, but in this case, since they were only doing one scene from the play, there was no director and they had rehearsed on their own. Result: disaster!

On another occasion, in a rather forgettable one-act comedy, the script called for the couple to tango the length of the stage, kiss passionately, and then tango back with their mouths clinging to each other. The audience began to laugh (as they were supposed to) with the start of the tango. With the kiss their laughter peaked and the hilarity was unrestrained. The only trouble was that the laughter proved infectious to the dancing, kissing couple. They started to laugh themselves, and the rest of the bussing trailed off into sloppy chaos. They were never able to get back into the play properly again.

A kiss, of course, is not the only thing which can go wrong during the actual performance of a play. We have previously discussed "staying in the play" and techniques the actor may use to do so. But there is another part of the problem which stems from what we might call "outside interference". Audience laughter affecting actors during a kiss is only one example of this.

The most common cause of such "outside interference" is the missed cue. It may have been missed by another actor, by the sound effects man, or the fellow working the lights, by the one in charge of raising and lowering the curtain, or the one who turns on or off the house lights. (One of the great lessons here is that the person in charge of the overall production should see to it that the most insignificant non-actors concerned with it know their cues backwards and forwards.) But the important thing about the missed cue is what do you, the actor, do about it?

The doorbell rings when it's not supposed to; the telephone doesn't ring when it is supposed to; the curtain drops in the middle of your second act closing speech; the curtain doesn't drop at the dramatic climax of the last act and you are left out there in full view of the audience; the first act opens on a darkened stage from which you are to deliver your lines and they are utterly drowned out by a clumsy usher and a tripping latecomer; your co-player mistakes one cue for another and by his response has propelled you into a later scene and you realize that you have left out half of the first act; the revolver doesn't go off when you fire it, but when you turn around to club your victim, it goes off in your face; you turn on the phonograph and turn back, arms wide to your partner, prepared to dance a poignant waltz, and no music is heard; you turn off the radio and a symphony blares; a dog's bark on cue is mysteriously heard as a cat's meow; you ring for the maid, and she never appears; you wait in the wings for the line which is your cue to enter and it is never delivered; you bend over and the seat of your pants splits—ah, yes, drama is like life, unpredictable, often embarrassing, always calling upon one to adapt quickly to impossible circumstances.

And adapting, of course, is the only answer. It is what the actor or actress *must* do. To have your wits about you onstage is an absolute must for every performance. To "keep one's cool," in the vernacular of the day, is often the only thing that can save the play.

The unexpected doorbell? Answer it; let the audience know that there is no one there; then go on with the play as if it never happened. Will the audience notice? Probably. But if it is simply dealt with—neither exaggerated, nor ignored—they won't dwell on it. If all else in the play works well, it will be forgotten.

The phone doesn't ring on cue? "I think I hear the phone," the actor might improvise. "I really should have it adjusted so it rings in this room too," he might observe before picking up the receiver and launching into the dialogue of the phone call.

The curtain that cuts your speech? Keep talking from behind it; project as loudly as you can in the hopes that the audience will be listening.

The curtain that doesn't drop and leaves you hanging? Freeze! And hope that the audience will think that the tableau is deliberate.

Latecomers that foul up your opening scene? Do what they do on Broadway. Ignore them. You can be sure that the audience will find its way into the play. Indeed, most plays are deliberately written so that the first five minutes contains nothing vital to the plot just because late arrivals are anticipated.

A "jump" mis-cue from a co-player? Snap judgment is really called for in this case. A decision must be made immediately. Either the dialogue must be left out in the hopes that the audience won't notice, or an effort must be made to insert a line which will cue the scene back to a point prior to where the jump was made. (The trouble with the second option is that the audience *will* notice the repetition. However, if the dialogue is crucial to the play, this price may have to be paid.) Whichever course you decide on, you must pursue it both quickly and forcefully enough to carry along your co-actor or co-actors. Nothing is more devastating than to have one performer intent on overcoming a goof by one strategy and another one pursuing an opposing strategy. Just as important as making the decision is knowing when your ego must give way in the face of a decision made by another actor on the stage.

The missing or mis-timed sound effects—the gun that doesn't go off, or goes off at the wrong time, the music that isn't heard when it should be and is heard when it shouldn't, the meow instead of a bark, or the roar instead of a whine—are, in dramaturgical terms, Acts of God over which the player has no control, the results of a Kismet to which he must ever be subject. The proper timing and delivery of sound effects is one of the most difficult things to achieve in amateur theatre. It should almost be taken for granted that one or more will be fouled up in any given performance of any play. And the only thing the actor can do is to continue on as though the gaffe had never occurred.

The performer—maid or otherwise—who doesn't enter on cue? Improvise a covering line which will carry you off-stage to fetch the negligent player. "Why does Bridget never come when I ring? What can she be doing in the pantry? I shall simply have to see for myself."

And when you are due to make your entrance and your cue never comes? Enter anyway! Take it for granted that those on-stage have lost their way. Your appearance and the delivery of your lines may help them find it.

As to the split pants, or the dropped panties, or other embarrassments of that nature—Well it depends. If you are doing a comedy, then play the laugh for all its worth. (But if it is a *sophisticated* comedy, be careful not to let the "accident" deteriorate into burlesque.) And if you are doing a drama? Be philosophical. Sit on it if possible. Be consoled by the knowledge that even this shall pass away. And go on with the play. Always go on with the play!

The play, after all, is the first responsibility of the actor. The second responsibility is to his fellow troopers. And this second responsibility is, perhaps, even more tricky than the first.

The interrelationship of the actors, the effect each has on the other, affects the play from the very first line reading. We have already discussed the problems this presents to the director and how he may cope with them in the initial stages of casting and rehearsal. Now we should consider it from the actor's point of view.

Presumably the director has weeded out the obvious

problems—the personality conflicts, the long-time antagonisms, etcetera. What you, the performer, are left with is the strength or weakness of your own ego vis-a-vis the ego of the people with whom you are playing. (Incidentally, it is important to realize here that although "ego" may take on negative connotations in the following discussion, it is also the thing which made you and your co-performers take to the amateur stage in the first place.) The very meaning of a scene may change according to these strengths and weaknesses. Yours will affect your fellow actors, and theirs will affect you.

What do you do when you find yourself overwhelmed onstage by another performer? The first thing to do, of course, is to consult with the director. His overall view of the play is more encompassing than yours, and therefore more valid. He may have made the decision to let you be overwhelmed for the sake of the play. If this is the case, there is nothing for you to do, given the spirit of the enterprise, but accept it.

There are times, however, when a director is aware of such a problem, does not condone it, but confesses himself unable to alter the situation. This is when your know-how as an actor becomes important. If the person you are playing opposite is upstaging you, then be aware of the positioning and try to alter it by your movements. If it helps the situation (i.e. puts the characters into a better dramatic balance), as noted before, the director will probably accept your revision of the blocking.

If the other actor overplays and you feel that you are lost in his or her shadow, do not give in to the temptation to out-shout, or out-strut, or out-perform. That is not the way to deal with it. A better idea is to get very soft when the overplayer gets loud, to sit very still when he strides back and forth across the stage, to portray your emotions subtly when he is parading his broadly. The difference in range between the two of you will become so apparent that either the director will tone down the overplayer's performance, or he will be forced to tone it down himself.

As a general rule, the stronger performer will set the tone for any given scene. But strength may not be obvious. A widening of the eyes may be more effective than a shriek, one tear more effective than wailing, a small hand gesture more effective than tearing up the scenery. There was a time in community theatre when the broad gesture was considered a must and reliance on facial expressions was thought only to have validity in movies where the close-up camera could catch them. Such is no longer the case. Improvements in lighting and the seating arrangements of the three-quarter or full round allow for much greater subtlety. And styles in theatre have changed so that audiences reject the broad approach to acting.

In a nutshell, to be on the safe side in drama, underplay.

But underplay does not mean to ignore dramatic points, lose pace, or weaken the vocal line. Emotion, but controlled emotion, is necessary in drama. It is, however, unnecessary for the actor to actually experience an emotion in order to portray it, the "method"—improperly understood—to the contrary. It is, in fact, dangerous. When professional actors appear to be carried away by the power of the scene they are playing, they are actually in strict control of their own emotions and are acting, not feeling the situation. The fact that the audience believes them is a tribute to their ability to assume and portray a character not their own and to impart to the audience emotions not their own but those of that character.

I knew a famous actress who bragged that she possessed such a technique that she could move an audience to tears while at the same time making gestures, unseen except by her fellow actors, which were calculated to break them up! And she once proved it to win a bet! Later she explained. "An actor's feelings are in a sense real, but imaginatively real, and spring only from a stage life the actor is living."

And Lee Strasberg reminds us that "this imaginative or stage feeling begins with a basis of remembered experience," which is the basis of his and Stanislavsky's method.

Some community theatre actors have not learned to live this imaginative life, and in their zeal they become so involved in the stage situation and the plight of the characters they are playing that they break down and find themselves weeping and sobbing. At first the audience is moved, but as soon as it senses that the actor has lost control and is struggling to regain enough composure to go on with the scene, it becomes embarrassed, forgets the play and is more interested in the actor's unfortunate situation. Usually the actor is rescued by another player who then has the difficult task of regaining the concentration of the audience.

When an experienced actor sheds tears, and the audience sees them course down his cheeks, you may be sure that the actor has planned just where his weeping begins and ends. He is "acting"

Playwright Paul Zindel wrote some really juicy parts for actresses in *The Effect of Gamma Rays on Man-in-the-Moon Marigolds* (above) and *And Miss Reardon Drinks a Little* (below). *(Picture above courtesy of Long Island Studio Theatre, Lindenhurst, N.Y. Picture below courtesy of Waterloo Community Playhouse, Waterloo, Iowa.)*

weeping. His tears are dominated by his will, and are as controlled as water running from a faucet which he can turn on or off.

Only once in my long experience have I seen a great actor "feel" the scene he was playing to such a degree that he came close to the limit of control. That was when Victor Moore played The Starkeeper in a revival of *Carousel*. He had been in retirement for several years and at first he insisted that he was too old to act again. We finally convinced him that he had to play at City Center so that the young theatregoers who had missed his many magnificent Broadway performances could see him live on stage. He was splendid, and just right in the role.

However, on opening night, when he came to the final touching scene and started his speech about life to the graduating class, with Billy Bigelow sent back from heaven to see his daughter graduate, Victor's voice broke, tears flooded from his eyes and he came so close to being overcome that for a split second I was afraid he would not be able to continue. But almost before I realized it, he had regained control and was proceeding in his strong but quavering voice, while the audience gulped, sobbed and blew its many noses. Even the critics were damp-eyed as they left the theatre on their way to write their rave reviews.

Victor was always completely natural on the stage, but when we say that of an actor we mean that he is giving an illusion of natural behavior and is using his technique in such a way that everything he does *seems* natural to us. He is at ease and aware of what he is doing and the effect he is creating every moment. Pacing, timing—especially for laughs—are not "natural." Actually, everything on the stage is artificial, but must give the illusion of reality. The greater the illusion, the greater the art.

Paradoxically, in achieving the illusion the actor must find a way to be in touch with his own emotions without losing control over them. Amateur actors, particularly, will find it most difficult to portray an emotion without feeling *something*. There are many techniques, born of many different schools of acting, for doing this.

Some actors find that violent exercise releases tension and allows emotion to flood in to fill the void. They take this exercise before the start of a scene which calls for a strong expression of emotion. They then pick and choose among those emotions to which they have opened themselves and select the one closest to that which is called for in the scene. Finally they concentrate on this emotion until they are called upon to release it onstage.

Other performers look to their own personal experience for the desired emotion. Is love called for? They close their eyes to summon up a vision of their own love object and the feelings which accompany it. Hatred? The process is repeated with the substitution of a vision of someone abhorent. Lust? Grief? Ambivalence? No matter the emotion, the technique is the same. But always with this proviso: It is a technique, and not an end in itself. Always the emotion must be a tool; the actor must control it; never the emotion the actor.

Still others seek the emotions in the performances of the other actors, accomplished and recognized actors they have seen on stage, or TV, or in films. They study how such an actor portrayed a particular emotion and try to emulate him or her. If this works for an amateur actor, there is no reason why it should not be done. However, one word of caution. Do not attempt to copy a professional actor in his portrayal of the actual part which you are playing. This is almost always fatal, if for no other reason than that the comparison is too direct and the audience will frequently view it as a burlesque.

Each actor must find his or her own emoting technique. If it works, then it is valid. That is the only test. As in all other facets of acting, your own experience will dictate the technique which is best for you. So it will be with serious emotions; so it will be with lighter ones. So it will be when playing drama, and so it will be with comedy.

In playing comedy, experience gives the actor an inner sense of timing. In the beginning, however, it is necessary to work out and plan for laughs that are more or less sure to come on certain lines and in certain situations. "Wait for your laughs" is just about the first thing actors have been taught since the year one.

Laughs are killed by talking through them and are stepped on by speaking before another actor's laugh has died out. When an actor gets an unexpected laugh and finds himself continuing with his next line, he must stop at once, let the laugh finish, and then begin his line again, sometimes repeating a word or two if necessary. The same is true if he begins to speak too quickly after another actor's line has unexpectedly brought a laugh. But to wait for a laugh that doesn't come is pretty awkward, too, and upsets the pace of the scene. It is all a matter of timing, and that is something learned only by experience, or supplied by an inner sensitivity and awareness on the part of the actor.

Knowing how to "build" a laugh, through facial expressions or body language, is another special talent that is often a birthright, but also something that can be acquired by constant attention and diligent practice. A good director can suggest ways for this, but while he is the actor's guide, he cannot be depended upon for every nuance of words and gestures. An actor must help himself by his own instinct and natural ability. If he goes too far, the director will stop him. If he does too little, the director will ask for more. A director and an actor work in tandem, one helping the other to achieve the desired results.

But the director cannot help the actor once he is on stage and the play begins. If the actor forgets a line he is alone. His immediate concern, however, should be not to let the audience know what has happened, and to remember not to panic. It is not the end of the world, or of the play. I once worked with a wonderful old actor who feared "going blank" (and he did, now and then) and I suggested that when that awful moment came, he should pick up a nearby object and examine it curiously, whether it be a book, an ash tray, anything at hand. It will seem to the audience like "a piece of business," and will fill in those otherwise agonizing few seconds until someone comes to the rescue with an improvised line, or the prompter supplies it from the wings, or the actor's own brain-computer goes to work again (usually the case). The audience may wonder why on earth that extraneous "piece of business" was necessary just then, but only a very few will realize the real predicament. Sometimes, as was previously discussed, it is necessary to ad lib.

Jose Ferrer has a collection of what he calls "nonsense lines" which he tells actors to use in these situations. One of them that I remember is, "Let us discuss that last statement. But first let us sit down and think about it for a minute or two." Joe says it fits just about any situation and makes the "ad libbing" which may be necessary less difficult. He also has a hilarious collection of poetic nonsense lines with no meaning whatsoever which he says sound just right when something goes wrong while playing the Bard.

Learning and remembering lines is easy for some players and immensely difficult for others. For the latter, it seems to me that the important thing is to thoroughly understand the character being played and the sort of things that character would say. It is good for both the memorizing of the lines and the playing of the role if the actor makes a list of what that character would be doing the night before rehearsal, for instance. Did he go to a party and stay late, or was he at home, looking at television? Does he like to watch romance, or violence, or a little of both? What does he like to eat? Or does he only like to eat what he has cooked for himself? Is his manner of dress gaudy or conservative? Does he take the bus or drive his own car? And so forth until the character becomes "real" as a child's imaginary playmate becomes real to him. Then the lines in the play will seem natural expressions of that personality and will be spoken by the actor as though he is thinking of them for the first time, which in a theatre sense he is. The actor has entered the skin of that character and is thinking as that character would.

When Robert Morley gave his magnificent performance as Oscar Wilde in the play of that name, everyone in the audience, including me, believed that Morley *was* Oscar Wilde and was saying

In costume dramas like *The Crucible*, amateur actors must be so completely at ease in their unaccustomed garb that it will not interfere with their performances. *(Picture courtesy of The Group Theatre, Rapid City, S.D.)*

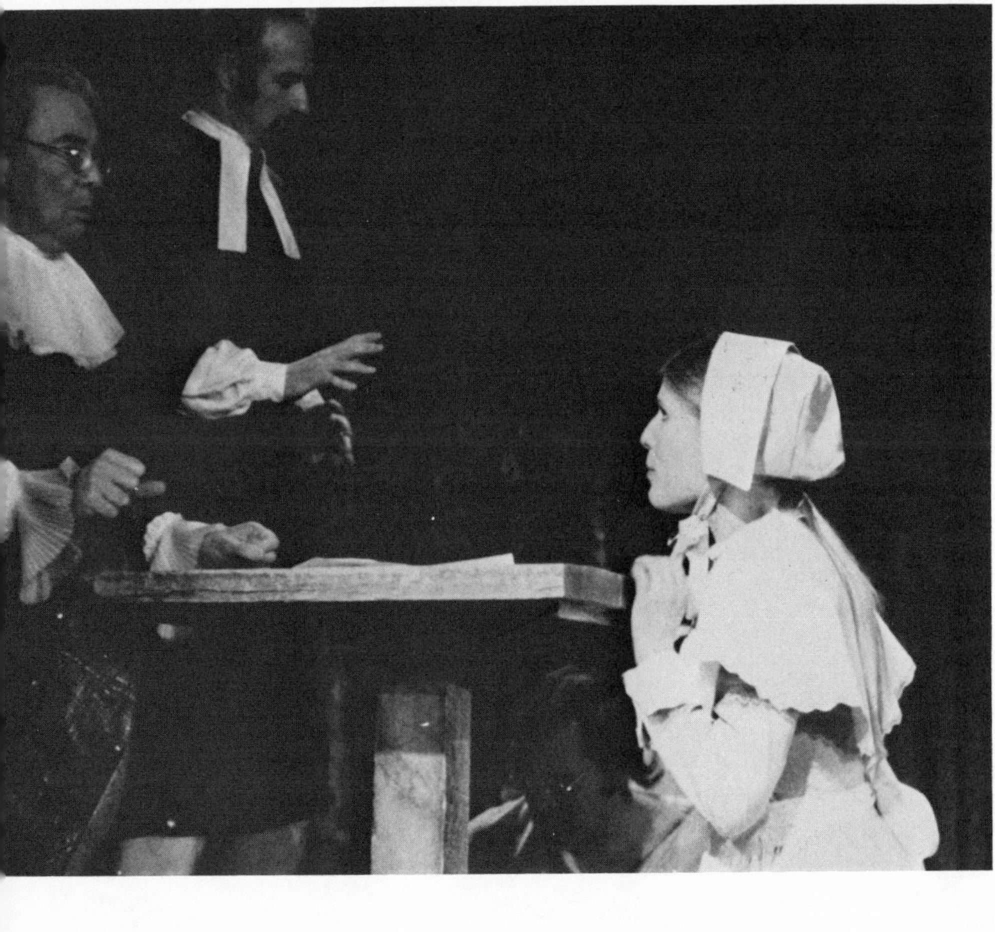

all those delightful witticisms on the spur of the moment. For me, Morley will always be Wilde and anyone who does not resemble him is an imposter!

But no successful actor, even Morley, ever loses his own personality in a role, and that is what makes him a star. In fact, some stars have not been really protean actors, but have played parts that suited them and their particular personality and appearance. Katharine Cornell *was* Elizabeth Browning in *The Barretts of Wimpole Street* just as Morley *was* Wilde, but she was always Katharine Cornell, too, and her husband and director carefully found other plays to "fit" her. Tallulah Bankhead played everything from Noel Coward's *Private Lives* to Tennessee Williams' *A Streetcar Named Desire*, and she was always terrific and always Tallulah.

On the other hand, players without that magic star quality, so admired by audiences and sought after by producers and managers, must acquire a chameleon-like ability to change and to become a character distinctly different from their own. That exercise of "making up" a character whom the actor gets to know and understand can be most helpful in community theatre work.

When the character has become real to the actor and the lines come easily, bringing a cassette recorder to rehearsals will help. Later at home, not only the words will be repeated, but the director's advice and instructions will be there, and stage positions will come to mind. Using stage positions as cues for lines is an old trick and a good one. But with some actors just never-ending repetitions of lines is the only way to get them to sink in and stay put.

If those "pieces of business," especially having to do several things at the same time while remembering the lines, are the bugaboos, practicing them at home until the actions become simultaneous and are subconsciously carried out, is a must. Then the lines that accompany the movements can occupy the conscious mind and be given their due importance on stage.

Being a good actor, a skillful actor, comes with experience, vigilance and concentration. It is hard work for some and just fun for others. In either case how soul-satisfying is the applause of the audience and the hugs and kisses of fellow performers when one's performance has just brought down the house!

chapter 6

Lighting

LET THERE BE LIGHT! the director calls out to the lighting designer, and the battle between them is on. Too many lighting designers ignore the objective of stage lighting, which is to let the audience see the faces of the actors as well as the general outline of their bodies and the beauties of the stage setting. Overly arty lighting can obscure rather than enhance these basic targets.

Lighting the actors' faces is important at all times, but it is especially important in comedies and musicals. In his zeal to make an artistic stage picture, however, the designer too often makes the scenery the star of the show. It may all look so pretty that nobody objects, and then when the audience does not respond with the expected laughter and applause, it is the director and the actors, sometimes even the play, that gets the blame. Full-up bright lighting is not the answer, either. Too much light flattens not only the actors' faces, but the entire stage picture and contributes a garish element that cheapens the action.

In contemporary theatre, more and more emphasis is on lighting. Plays which once called for many changes of scenery are now produced in a unit set with a flow of action which depends entirely on changes of position and changes of light. Directors who were trying to reproduce on stage the freedom of film sequences brought about this development in lighting and set designing techniques and it is being used with increasing skill each theatre season. *Annie* is a case in point. Still, right around the corner from *Annie* the revival of Rodgers and Hammerstein's *The King and I* is playing to sold-out houses in spite of the fact that the now old-fashioned tradition of "numbers in one"—songs or dances done downstage in front of a curtain while the main scene is being changed—is faithfully followed. If this were to happen in a new

Broadway musical, however, it undoubtedly would not find favor either with the critics or the theatregoers. The set and lighting designers—David Mitchell and Judy Rasmuson—of *Annie* keep the sets changing and the action progressing without interruption, and the production maintains the swift pace the increasingly impatient public demands of new works today.

The lighting designer for the community theatre is usually hampered in his efforts by the facilities with which he has to work and too small a budget. Nevertheless, very fine effects can be achieved with ingenuity and diligence. Just as the designers of the scenery and the costumes must have an understanding of the aims of the playwright and the director, so too must the lighting designer. The play must be read and re-read and the various scenes and dramatic or comic moments evaluated for their moods and atmosphere. Talks with the director and the set designer are essential, too, and attendance at rehearsals is helpful. Notes should be made of the time of day or night of each scene and whether any changes occur. Such designations as late afternoon with the sun setting, or evening with lamps lit changing later to a set lighted only with moonlight, or perhaps opening with a thunderstorm which suddenly ceases with a burst of bright sunlight, will all demand lighting notations.

In comedies where the "box set" of a room is used and the action takes place in a relatively short space of time, no change of lighting is necessary and as long as a good and properly focused supply of light is furnished—neither too bright nor too dim—with everything looking "natural," and no one conscious of the lighting, the result must be deemed successful. This can be achieved by simple means and inexpensive equipment. One word of caution though. If a facility is being used for the first time as a theatre, it is a good idea to bring in a local electrician to make sure that the necessary minimum amperage capacity of 30,000 watts is available for the dimmer board. This will avoid the aggravation and confusion of a series of blown fuses and other mishaps.

Footlights are being used less and less in the professional theatre and scarcely at all in community theatres. Still, they are useful for lighting musicals, and have been most helpful when older ladies depend upon flattering lighting to lend them youth. "*Surprise Pink* to be used in the footlights" was in the contracts Tallulah Bankhead signed for all her summer theatre engagements in her later years.

Basic lighting for small theatre groups can be obtained with only two lights if necessary. They are the 500 - 750 watt 6-inch Klieglight (above) and the 500 - 750 watt 6-3/8 inch Fresnel (right). *(Pictures courtesy of Kliegl Bros., Long Island City, N.Y., manufacturers and distributors of the equipment shown.)*

Surprise Pink is, as Tallulah knew, a helpful color; it is also a useful and warm color for general use. Much can be done with it and with other colored lights by an ingenious designer.

There often are existing footlights in old theatres taken over by a community group. But in a space with no footlights, it is just as well to forget about them, as they are expensive to buy and install and no real necessity.

Abe Feder, who is the dean of lighting designers in both the theatrical and architectural worlds, and also an outstanding set designer, was responsible for the scenery and lighting of many of the successful productions we presented at the New York City Center. His genius was clearly demonstrated when he transformed our borrowed set for *My Fair Lady*, which had seen years of use on Broadway and on tour, into a pristine thing of beauty with the magic of light. Feder had designed the lighting for the original Broadway production, so his hardware set-up remained more or less the same; it was his new choice of colors which made the difference.

Feder says that lighting a set is a form of painting. He first does the over-all background lighting for his "picture"—like a color wash, he puts it—and then he fills in the details, highlighting the playing areas and the forms and the faces of the actors. For highlighting faces he uses a minimum three inch Fresnel one hundred watt spotlight. For highlighting a figure at a door, or "shaping" it, he uses an ellipsoidal spotlight, which allows templating. Feder never lights without "bodies" on the stage. He says they do not have to be the actors who will be playing the parts, but stand-ins—easier to find in community theatres since unions are not involved—must be there.

Most small theatre groups must depend upon barely adequate lighting facilities. However, if the appointed designer has some knowledge of the "hardware" involved and some ingenuity and imagination for its use, excellent results are possible. It is also important for him to keep in mind that the lighting of the set is as important to the success of the play as any of the work being done by the actors, the director, the other designers, or anyone else involved.

Speaking of the "hardware" used for lighting in the community theatres, Feder says, "There are two standard work-horses: the six inch Fresnel, which can be focused from spot to flood, with throws of ten to twenty feet, and the ellipsoidal reflector spotlight, with its hard-edged beam and throws of twenty to fifty feet, depending on the lens systems within the piece of apparatus. These two lamps are still the most used, in spite of all the fancy new electronic inventions for lighting which have come into being in recent years. They can be placed on border pipes and vertical pipes, and I suggest that every small theatre would do well to install permanent vertical pipes from floor to ceiling on either side of the stage, about five feet apart, starting from the curtain line, or front line of the playing area. Not only the lamps can be clamped to these, but plug boxes and cables can be hung there, keeping them off the floor.

"I recommend that only rubber-covered cable be used, as it does not twist and therefore does not break, exposing wires, which can cause fire. Another safeguard is the use of twist-locks, which must be unlocked to separate cables, instead of the usual stage plugs which often flare up when they are pulled apart. All stage plugs, of course, should be the grounded or three-pronged plugs, which cannot gather electricity from other sources.

"Multiple plugging boxes should always be used to connect up cables on one side of the stage or the other, no matter how small the theatre. There should be one box stage right and another one stage left. Also, they should be kept off the floor, which is where the vertical pipe comes in handy. Hang them up, about three feet off the floor, and hang the cables up off the floor, too, as much as possible.

"Beam projectors were the old work-horses for simulating sunshine and other bright light at the back of the stage, but a new lamp has taken their place. This is the PAR 64 1000 watt lamp in either spot or flood. It gives off two and a half times more light than the old beam projector and lasts for four thousand hours. They are now available in PAR heads, which are long metal containers with louvre controls which take away all glare. They come in spotlight containers with clamps, and they, too, can be hung on those vertical pipes—the ones nearest the back of the stage.

"Real theatrical lighting equipment should always be used and should bear the UL (Underwriters Laboratory) label, which insures its quality and its safety. This equipment cannot be purchased at the local hardware stores, or lighting fixture distributors, but it can be ordered by them from the proper theatrical supply houses.

"I am very much against the use of house extension cords and house dimmers, the kind that are available for home use. They are not built to carry the load required for stage lighting and can be dangerous. Theatrical dimmers are best for your purpose. They should be 12-bank, 2,500 watt auto-transformer units, having a total capacity of 30,000 watts and using a power capacity of 200 amperes. Each dimmer will have a method of plugging in for individual lamps, making possible the use of 48 separate circuits. You will not use more than 18,000 watts at one time, but can replug between scenes. The important thing is the fail-safe quality of the board. When overloaded, the circuit breaker trips off and protects the dimmer.

"Avoid using the old-fashioned arc spotlight. It is a fire hazard of the worst kind. If a follow spot is needed for a musical or a revue, the one I prefer is the Kliegl, which does not get hot. The Kliegl follow-spot has a sixteen inch lens, with a 1000 watt lamp, and it has enormous brilliance. Its light beam can be shaped and focused. It can be put on a stand and used from a platform at the back of a room or auditorium with no danger of fire because it is an incandescent lamp. Arc spotlights are dangerous. Do not accept one even if it is offered as a gift. The Kliegl is expensive to buy, but it can be rented when needed. And it is safe!

"Another new and excellent development is the small quartz three hundred watt border light, which is particularly fine for lighting backgrounds or cycloramas. They should be hung in four to six foot border sections about five feet from the cyc as a back border light and they will illuminate the whole cyclorama beautifully.

"Leaving the area of hardware, let me mention a few lighting situations to which newcomers to the art of lighting will soon become accustomed:

"When the light level of the cyclorama or backdrop is set against the brilliance of the eye, as the first and correct step, you then fill in from your first pipe area lighting. The last thing you bring up is the front lighting for faces and revealment. Now a strange thing happens. Your cyc or backdrop will darken. Naturally, you then increase the brilliance of the cyc to counteract the brilliance in front.

"When lighting back wall windows, you start as you do with the cyc, then bring up your area lighting inside, then your front lighting and again you must bring up the outside lighting.

"When you shoot beams of light into a room through a side window, you will find that you have created a piece of sculpture; i.e., the highlighted furniture, person, or persons. This looks interesting, but we can't play a scene in that light unless you are thinking of extremely dramatic action. So, again, your first pipe area will have to be brought up and the front lights also to fill in for visibility of the actors and their faces.

"As a last word, remember that colored lights change not only the colors of the set, but the color and texture of the material of the costumes."

It should be added, for the benefit of the community theatre novice, that there are three basic means of achieving color in lighting. The simplest, but also the least flexible, is the use of colored bulbs in spotlights. You should be aware, however, that the color burns off the bulb very quickly. This makes sense in a situation where you have fixed lighting for the length of the play, or at least for the length of one act of the play (if you don't mind changing bulbs between the acts), and where you are using at least eight lights in two stationary banks (vertically as described, or horizontally from above). In such a situation, you can experiment by mixing colored bulbs with your usual lighting and when you find the desired effect, simply stick with it. Since the color availability from bulbs is apt to be quite basic, you should keep in mind the lighting truths of the three basic colors as follows: yellow softens, red warms (is sexy) and blue isolates (lends distance and eerieness).

The second means of achieving color is by the use of gels. These are simply heat resistant forms of colored plastic which fit over the lenses of spotlights. They come in a much greater variety of colors than bulbs do, and can therefore provide much more subtlety in color lighting. They can also be changed much more easily and if your lights are accessible, it is not much trouble to turn down a spot and quickly replace one gel with another. You do not have to remove the lens as you do to change a bulb. Feder cautions not to use heavy primary gelatins, but light tints that are either warm or cool and will not make the actors look unnatural.

The most versatile instrument for color lighting is the color wheel. This is a wheel which can be positioned directly in front of a spotlight and rotated so that from four to eight lens-sized gels can instantaneously alter the color of the lighting. For moods and subtle shadings, a color wheel is indispensible. Every community theatre group should have at least two. (Two, rather than one, in order to blend the projected color light rays.) If you can't afford to buy them, they can be rented from Times Square Theatrical and Studio Supply Corporation.

"Lighting in the theatre is part and parcel of the emotional experience shared by the artists on stage and the audience out front on opening night," concludes Feder.

It is a definition to be pondered by community theatre members. If there is ever a surplus of ticket sale money, one of the first priorities on which to spend it should be proper lighting equipment. For that time, when it comes, here are three dependable suppliers of stage lighting and equipment:

Kliegl Brothers
32-32 48th Avenue
Long Island City, N.Y. 11101
Tel.: (212) 786-7474

Times Square Theatrical and
Studio Supply Corporation
318 West 47th Street
New York, N.Y. 10036
Tel.: (212) 245-4155

Altman Stage Lighting Company, Inc.
57 Alexander Street
Yonkers, N.Y.
Tel.: (212) LO 9-7777 and (914) 476-7987

Dramatic lighting focuses the attention in this scene from ***The Effect of Gamma Rays on Man-in-the-Moon Marigolds.*** ***(Picture courtesy of Long Island Studio Theatre of Lindenhurst, N.Y.)***

chapter 7

The Setting

EVERY THEATRICAL PRODUCTION has a setting, with the rare exceptions of plays which are written for a bare stage. The setting, or scenery, is designed, constructed and lit to define as nearly as possible the place, and the time, of the events taking place, and to some extent to convey the mood or quality of the playwright's theme.

When the curtain rises, or the lights go up, on a setting which shows a living-room in a Connecticut upper-class home, furnished with fine early American furniture, sunlight streaming into the room through large windows, beyond which can be seen a garden with colorful flowers, the audience is likely to break into applause, to signal its appreciation of the work of the designers of the setting and the lighting. The atmosphere for the play they have come to enjoy has been established for them; they recognize and empathize with the locale. But as soon as the actors appear and the action starts, the set itself is properly forgotten, relegated to the subconscious.

A setting which distracts the attention of the audience from the substance of the play, or gives a misleading or incorrect point of view, is the *bete noire* of playwrights, directors and creative producers. Fortunes have had to be spent by professional theatre companies in re-designing and rebuilding scenery which was seen to be wrong during out-of-town tryouts, or even during preview performances on Broadway. It is not possible to point out the specifics to avoid. Too often it is an element that looked right on paper that turns into such a visual disaster on stage.

For instance, there once was a musical with an important star, a lovely score and a weak book. In other words, it was a musical that needed everything going right for it. During the tryout, it seemed to gather momentum and growing approval by the audience during the first act, only to lose it all during the intermission and have to start all over again with the beginning of the second act. The director finally came to the conclusion that it happened because the beautifully designed and draped grey velvet show curtain came down on the first act like a cascade of wet cement, with an equivalently damping effect on the audience. After hours of loudly asserted disbelief by the designer, and acrimonious debate between him and the director, the curtain was replaced at a great cost by one of similar design made in pale pink chiffon. The curtain itself received applause the first time it was used, and the director said he could tell by the lighthearted chatter and laughter in the lobby during intermission that the second act would get off to a good start. And so it did. After some other minor changes the show came to Broadway and became a solid hit.

Designing for the community theatre is like the stories that start, "There's good news and bad news." The good news is that since most of the plays and shows done in those theatres have been professional successes, the original designers have ironed out whatever difficulties the script presented. Also, both the Samuel French and the Dramatists Play Service "acting verions" that are apt to be used as scripts furnish photographs of the finished production as well as detailed floor plans, showing entrances, windows, and the placement of furniture. Also included are a "furniture and property lot" which lists, for instance:

Carpet on stage. Curtains at windows as desired.
Pictures and electric wall brackets on the walls.
1 large divan, with cushions (down center)
1 chair (right of divan)
1 chair (down right, below the door. See floor plan.)

Also there usually is a "hand prop plot" which goes like this:

First Act:
Jimmy. 2 Tennis rackets. Cigarette case. Lighter.
Margaret. (second entrance) Lipstick.
Kitty. Handbag. Gloves.

Second Act:
Stage: Playing cards. Bridge scoring pad and pencil.
(On table above divan)

Coffee table and tray of tea things for two persons. (Ready off stage left.)
Personal:
Jimmy. Cigarette case, filled. Lighter.

Usually there is also a "lighting plot" which is also helpful;

Act 1
Front lights on balcony. Six 400 watt reflectors.
Colors in same. Four have No. 6 straw and 112 pink.
Two have No. 8 amber and 114 pink.

Then there are "sound effects plots" that go something like this:

Act 1.
Door-bell.
Telephone bell.
Door-slam.
Glass-crash and shouting.

So the set designer, light designer, property man and sound man have much of their work done for them, although not every Samuel French and Dramatists Play Service script has all of this help. But I have yet to see an "acting version" from either publisher without that detailed floor plan and the production photographs, as well as a pretty complete description of the set or sets at the beginning of each act.

Now the bad news is that all too often the original designs are not at all suitable for the playing area of the theatre in question, and whole new conceptions are called for. Also, when the play being produced is a classic and the "script" is from the director's library, there usually is only the playwright's narrative description as a guide. All of Bernard Shaw's descriptions are delightful reading, but less than helpful to the designer. Ibsen is a little better, but still it is description which must be made tangible and that can pose a problem for the community theatre designer. Add to this the usual budget limitations and inadequate working conditions and the bad news is complete.

Simplicity is the keynote to good design, whether it is for a million dollar Broadway musical or a little theatre with a minimal budget. I doubt if there has been a play or musical ruined by underproduction, but there have been many fatally over-produced. Too ornate scenery, and costumes too colorful, too detailed and too gimmicky, have smothered many a pretty good show. On the other hand, there have been some extremely cluttered sets which were so right that once the audience recognized them for what they were and what they were conveying, the details were ignored and the enjoyment of the play was genuinely enriched by them.

One such was the extraordinary setting for the short-lived *American Buffalo*, which won the 1977 *Tony* for designer Santo Loquasto's junk shop with its thousand and one small props stashed away on shelf after shelf that covered two-thirds of the stage. The action took place on the one-third that was down-stage, in front of the shelves, which were forgotten after they had drawn their salvo of admiring applause. In this case the clutter served a valid dramatic purpose directly related to the play.

There was also the extraordinary setting for *Brief Lives*, the one-man play in which British actor Roy Dotrice so skillfully portrayed the last day in the life of John Aubrey in his London lodgings of the 1600's. British designers had assembled about one thousand props of authentic antique vintage and artfully arranged them in their conception of a room that had been lived in and not properly cleaned or dusted for decades. Mr. Dotrice displayed and handled many of these articles as he told his old man's tales of his life during Elizabethan days. (His favorite prop was an ornate chamber pot which he used, slightly off-stage but with sound effects, and then emptied out the window into the street.)

During the one intermission, Mr. Dotrice's John Aubrey napped in a comfortable chair on stage, and with the house lights up a good portion of the audience at each performance came down to the footlights to inspect and discuss the setting and its fantastic furnishings. But once the house lights dimmed, all attention again was riveted on John Aubrey.

In each case—*American Buffalo* and *Brief Lives*—the picture the designers chose to present was detailed and complete and the viewers more than satisfied with it. So, if a play calls for an unusual setting with a plethora of properties, it is important for the community theatre designer to make it authentic. If he does not, the audience becomes subconsciously aware that something is wrong and its attention falters.

Most plays call for the simplest frame for a realistic interior. This is the usual "box," or three-walled room. A few plays need an exterior, which usually is a painted cyclorama with set pieces (trees, shrubs, etc., painted and constructed to stand by them-

Settings, not necessarily realistic, can be designed to heighten the dramatic effect desired. In *The Music Man*, the train was obviously not real. But its very unreality enhanced the feeling of a time when bonhommie among traveling salesmen could lead to group singing. *(Picture courtesy of Baton Rouge Little Theater Inc., Baton Rouge, La.)*

The use of a scrim in *Heaven Can Wait* conveyed the ethereal nature of dead characters who could observe the action of a love scene without being seen by those in the scene. *(Picture courtesy of Stagecrafters of the Jewish Community Center, Cincinnati, Ohio.)*

Most community theatres furnish their sets by borrowings from local merchants or from people's homes. They should set a mood as the deer head and guns on the wall do in *Oldest Living Graduate* (above) and the family-style appurtenances do in *Spofford* (below). *(Picture above courtesy of Midland Community Theatre, Inc., Midland, Texas. Picture below courtesy of Ann Arbor Civic Theatre, Ann Arbor, Mich.)*

selves). But besides these two fundamentals there are many design opportunities, depending on the director's and designer's creativity, and limited only by the subject matter of the play or show and, of course, the playing area available.

When a "bare stage" is asked for by the playwright, it is not as simple or as empty as it sounds. *Our Town* has often been hailed as the first play in modern times to be presented on a bare stage. But although there was no back drop or other painted scenery on the stage, there were properties: a ladder that John could climb to look out of his imaginary bedroom window toward Emily's room in her home across the way; a board across two chair backs where John and Emily sipped their drinks at the imaginary soda fountain, and, of course, the rows of chairs that held Emily and the others after their deaths in the "graveyard" of the final act. So vivid is imagination that I seem to remember a standing trellis with flowering vines, but Jed Harris, who produced and directed Thornton Wilder's lovely play, never would have stooped to using anything so realistic.

Leaving much to the imagination of the audience is useful when the designer is working out the scenery for a fantasy, or a play with several changes of scenes. Platforms of different levels against a plain backdrop can, with proper lighting and costumes, create the mood, atmosphere and locale of many scenes. Or a background of handsome draperies, with an inset window, door, or mantel, can make a richer effect when the proper furnishings are provided.

Screens, too, are useful for scene changes. They are easy and inexpensive to make and can be carried on and off stage in a trice. Frames of light wood are simply covered with canvas or muslin and can be hinged together and painted or decorated to represent the needed locations or backgrounds. They are especially appropriate for small musicals and revues, as they lend themselves to imaginative ornamentation.

When designing the "box" or interior setting which will not be changed during the play, the first consideration should be paid to the proper entrances, doors or arches, and the sources of the necessary light. Then there is the predominant color to be decided upon. Drab colors are effective for drama. Latex paint, by the way, comes in just about every color imaginable and is simple to use. Stencil designs are available which can be applied for decoration.

When it comes to furnishing the interior "box" or room, all the necessary props can almost always be borrowed. Scrounging for props is a favorite game with almost all community theatre designers and property men. Neighbors like to see their possessions on stage. Shopkeepers can almost always be induced to furnish all kinds of paraphernalia on loan in exchange for program credit and a pair of tickets. (Point out to them that it's not only good publicity, it's good community relations.) Paintings for the walls, plants, bric-a-brac, carpets, curtains, draperies and cushions never need to be bought.

There are some things to avoid. Mirrors are one. They reflect the stage lighting into the eyes of the audience as well as the actors. If a mirror is an essential property, something that is commented upon or used in a scene, it should be soaped or otherwise lightly coated to prevent the glare and reflection from causing distractions. Tin or aluminum are sometimes used for mirrors, but they never look right. Unless a mirror is absolutely vital to the play, it is better to do without it.

One thing never to forget is that while simplicity is not always easy to achieve in stage design, it should always be the target. When in doubt, it will always turn out best for the play if the setting is under-produced rather than buried by the intemperance of a designer who couldn't decide when enough was enough.

Simple cutout scenery works well with children's plays like *The Clown Who Ran Away* by Conrad Seller. *(Picture courtesy of the Studio Playhouse, Upper Montclair, N.J.)*

chapter 8

Costumes

WHATEVER AN ACTOR is wearing when he makes his first entrance helps him to immediately establish the character he will be developing during the course of the play. The color, cut, even the material of his costume, all tell us something about that character. If he is wearing a loud plaid suit, trousers too tight and shoulders too broad, tie and pocket handkerchief clashing, and two-tone shoes, before he says his first word on stage we say, "Ah, this is going to be a brash, loud-mouth, probably with some of the play's amusing lines." If it is a girl who comes on and she is in a neat suit, plain blouse and sensible shoes, we are alerted that she is the efficient secretary of the leading man and, when she takes off her glasses and unpins her tight little chignon, she will turn out to be the girl he loved all along. (The play will doubtless please the public at the preview performances and the critics will probably murder it when it opens.) The middle-aged man, in heavy tweeds, not too well pressed, smoking a pipe? "A country gentleman; probably a writer," the audience guesses. This kind of costuming is not only accepted by the audience and the critics, but expected.

It is this descriptive part of the designers' art which has brought about the use of the word "costume" to describe whatever it is actors are wearing on stage. One never hears of "clothes" for a play.

Imagination, taste, knowledge, insight and showmanship make up the costume designer's talent whether he is outfitting the cast of a community theatre play, a Broadway musical, or an off-Broadway showcase. Of course, the matter of budget limits the amateur designer, but the same opportunity exists to make an important contribution to the total picture that the director, the actors and all the other talents involved, are blending to make the play come alive for the public.

To a large extent, costume is character, and the costume designer may have as much to do with a successful portrayal as does the actor. The costumes tell us right away that it was a different time with different morals in Tennessee Williams's *Summer and Smoke* (above). *(Picture courtesy Ann Arbor Civic Theatre, Ann Arbor, Mich.)* In *Beckett* (below), the threat that the swords will be used is implicit from the very beginning in the macho garb of all but the victim. *(Picture courtesy of Delray Beach Playhouse, Delray Beach, Fla.)*

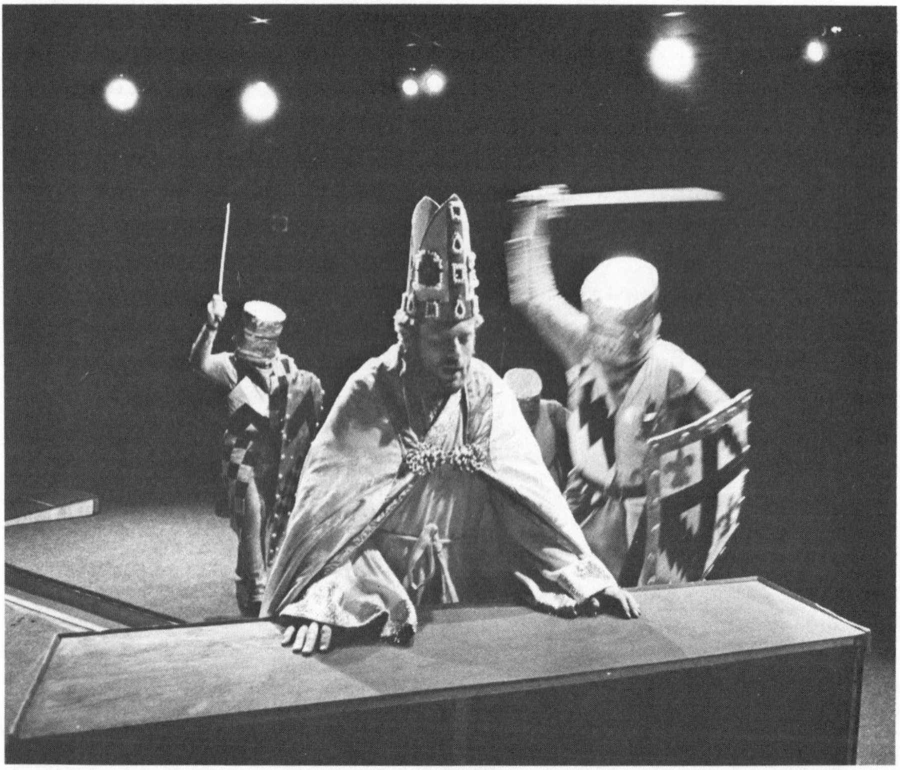

How does the costume designer begin? First and foremost, before the designer so much as picks up a pencil or a pair of scissors, he must read and re-read the play. He must become thoroughly acquainted with not only the play's characters, but with the playwright's theme and subject matter; also the time, place, even the weather, and the mood of the various scenes. Then, after talks with the director and the set designer, he begins to outline his work. He makes a list of the names of the characters, the scenes they are in, and the type of outfits he must furnish for each of them: day-time, evening, plain, dressy, or in more detail as the spirit moves him.

Before he goes too far, he should know the color scheme the set designer has in mind. One of the reasons for the inevitable frantic rush to get costumes to the actors on time is often due to the indecision of the set designer about the colors he will use, colors not only for the setting, but for all the properties: the paintings, rugs, upholstery, pillows, draperies, even the ash-trays. The costume designer wants to design or—the usual case in community theatres—select costumes that not only will go with the setting, but at the same time will stand out in contrast to the colors used. Costumes for the leading players must be striking enough to keep them from fading into the general background, yet not clash. Often the final decision is reached by not only the set and costume designers, but the director.

The director makes another early and essential contribution to costume design when he decides on the period for his production. Directors sometimes change the original time period in which the action of a classic or standard play takes place by several decades, or even by a century or so. In the case of plays written in the '20's and '30's, the director may feel that the subject matter is just as pertinent today as it was back then, so why not put it in a contemporary setting? In this case the community theatre designer's work is lessened since modern clothes can be used and the actors can furnish their own wardrobes.

If the director decides to keep the play in its original '20's or '30's setting, then those trunks in the attic or in the cellar-bin, with their collections of clothes that were too treasured to throw away will come in handy. Often suits and dresses need no more than a bit of fitting and a good pressing. Sometimes, because they are now to be used in larger-than-life situations, dyeing more vivid colors or adding more elaborate trimmings may be necessary. But since simplicity is always best, it is more likely that frills will be removed rather than added.

Scrounging for costumes is as necessary for community theatre costume designers as it is for set designers and property people. But if any clothes are borrowed, period or modern, special care must be taken with them; the actors must be cautioned to handle them carefully, and when they are to be returned they must be cleaned and pressed. Then the same source will be available another time.

If proper period costumes cannot be borrowed, then it becomes necessary to sit down and make them. Renting them would be simpler, but that is expensive and too often the results are unsatisfactory.

Researching fashion magazines of the period, available in most libraries, will furnish ideas to the costume designer. The simplest and best-looking should be selected. Then sketches can be made and patterns cut from them. It is not always necessary, however, to start from scratch. Standard patterns from the leading dressmaker pattern companies can be adapted by a designer who is skillful with a pair of shears. From these patterns inexpensive muslins should be cut, fitted and basted before tackling the material for the finished product. In this way costly blunders or miscalculations can be avoided, and when the actual work of sewing the costume together begins, it will proceed very swiftly. There is no need, of course, for handsewn seams and hems and other niceties of the needle since "distance lends enchantment" to the view of the audience. There are many short cuts that save time and patience in this work. They are spelled out in any number of dressmaker manuals.

When it comes to ornate outfits for "costume plays," which are produced as a rule around the holidays, the styles can be researched in illustrated books of the period, and the silhouette of the time carefully studied. If the silhouette is properly achieved, and the proper materials selected, everything else can be considered as additions or decorations and treated as such. No hand-done embroidery is needed, of course. Sewn-on passementerie (beaded or spangled lace) is effective, as are cut-out designs from pretty prints which are quickly glued, pasted or ironed on the basic fabric. Designs can be painted on, too, either stencilled or applied freehand.

Nylon is less expensive than silk and is even more effective on stage, also easier to handle. Cotton velveteen gives a fine rich effect and with a bit of gold braid and the jeweled trimming that comes

Outlandish make-up enhances the effect of Mrs. Malaprop's costume in *The Rivals*, and helps establish her personality. *(Picture courtesy Kalamazoo Civic Players, Kalamazoo, Mich.)*

by the yard and can be quickly basted on where most effective, raiment fit for stage royalty materializes with all the required splendor but without undue travail or cost.

When hoop-skirts are to be used, muslin skirts with the proper size hoops should be furnished for rehearsals so the actresses can get used to them. They are difficult to handle and can cause embarrassment if they suddenly fly up in back or in front, revealing period underdrawers. (In *The King and I*, the Siamese ladies have that difficulty the first time they dress in western garb for Mrs. Anna's party for the British Ambassador. In that particular case they were wearing no drawers at all, but only the Ambassador has that view, to his astonishment. But this, of course, was deliberate.)

If the costumes have trains which must be picked up for dancing, or allowed to trail for an important entrance, these also must be furnished for rehearsals, as well as any long heavy skirts which might be tripped on. Corsets must be gotten used to, also, if the small waistline of our great-grandmothers is the aim of the designer.

In the case of all costume plays it is essential for the designer to know which actors must make quick and agile movements, so that the costumes for them will allow the necessary freedom for duels, jousts, tumbling or dancing. Leotards or body stockings for both men and women can be the basis for endless variations of costumes for these active roles. Decorated doublets, jerkins and short capes allow ease of movement for the men, and the designer's imagination can run rampant in devising light but effective outer garments for the ladies.

Designing for dancers is an art in itself, but the community theatre designer can be successful if he will keep in mind that not only freedom of movement is necessary, but that the beauty of the line of his design when the dancer is in motion can add value to the dance itself. Also, fitting to the dancers' bodies is important. While comfort has top priority in all costuming, for dancers it is essential.

On the subject of comfort, more than the physical must be taken into consideration. Imagine the discomfort of the actress in a tight, short skirt which rides up about her knees each time she must sit down and face the audience. She is forced to clamp her knees tight together and keep them that way to avoid interest centering on her inner thighs! A similar problem occurs if she has to wear a gown cut so low in front that she dare not bend over for fear of exposure!

Even above comfort and skill of the design, actors must feel that they are putting on the characters they play when they put on

Costumes don't just establish period, they can also establish locale, as in *Flower Drum Song. (Picture courtesy Downey Civic Light Opera Assoc., Downey, Calif.)*

The costume designer must always make the choice between realism and stylization. The latter was decided upon in this production of *Androcles and the Lion. (Picture courtesy of The Group Theatre, Rapid City, S.D.)*

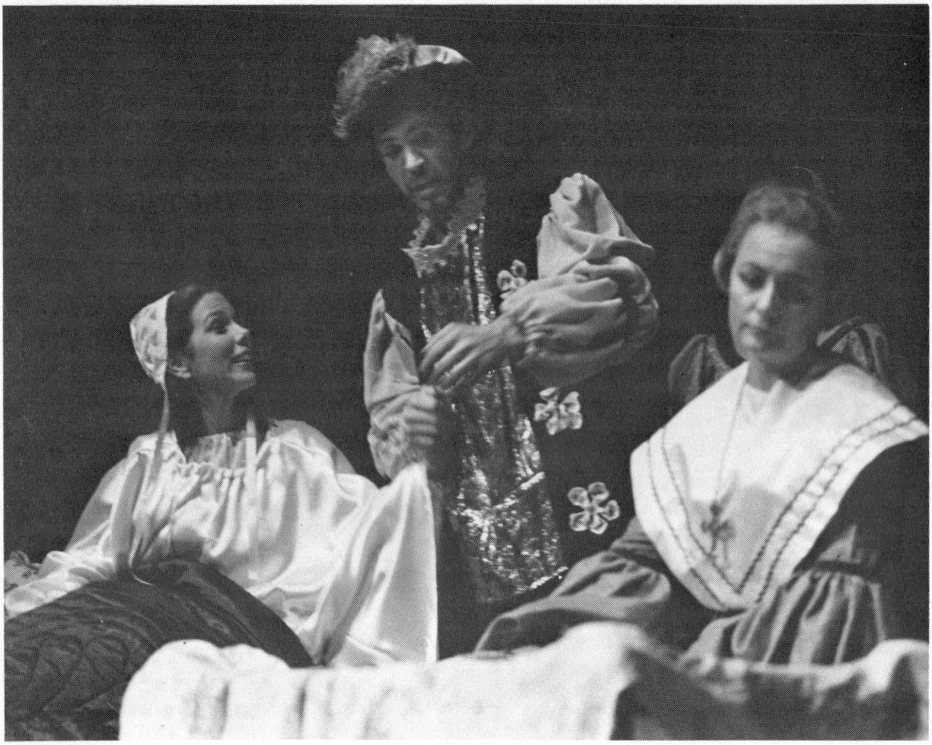

Some costumes must be especially created, as in *Anne of the 1,000 Days* (above), while others may be found by scrounging in the attic for old clothes, or old uniforms, as was the case with *Shield Head* by Jonas Arnason (below). *(Picture above courtesy of the Wyandotte Community Theatre, Allen Park, Mich. Picture below courtesy of the Midland Community Theatre, Inc., Midland, Texas.)*

their costumes. They must first and always like themselves in them and be eager to show themselves in them. The actress playing a fascinating *femme fatale* will carry off the role with aplomb if she has a gorgeous outfit, even though we know that she is a rather plain housewife who has never so much as shared an ice cream soda with any man other than her husband. The local prankster and hale-fellow-well-met will convince his best friends that he is a stern and pompous magistrate if he makes his entrance in the properly austere and forbidding costume, made of dark, stiff and unyielding material.

If quick changes are to be made, one piece garments which open completely down the back or front are convenient. Snaps, hooks-and-eyes, zippers and, above all, buttons, are usually avoided. Sometimes very large—at least half an inch in diameter—snaps come in handy. Zippers seem a good idea but often get stuck at just the wrong moment. Velcro, that fastening material that presses together and holds tight until it is pulled apart in the proper way, is heaven-sent. Men's costumes are always extremely difficult to arrange for quick changes. Usually the basic outfit remains the same and only accessories are changed.

In any case, for both men and women, helpers must be on hand when the changes are being made. In community theatre, it is often best to just avoid plays—especially costume plays—that have tricky changes.

When the production has finished its engagement, whoever is in charge of the costumes should see that they are returned to their owners, or if made on the premises, put carefully away, after they have been cleaned. They can be hung on racks, if there is room for racks, and the racks covered with large dust-proof cloths. Or they can be put in boxes, layered with plenty of tissue paper, and the boxes carefully marked. All the accessories should be included in the box with each costume.

If wigs have been used, they should be cared for, brushed, combed and set, before being stored. They are expensive, but do add dimension to a character when used, especially in costume plays. In contemporary plays, the actress's own hair should be styled for the part whenever possible.

Period shoes should be stuffed with tissue paper or put on shoetrees before being put away. Men's period shoes are always a problem, by the way, but adding buckles to modern shoes helps in many cases. It is wise to have the local shoemaker take care of any changes made, however, to avoid the embarrassment of the additions falling off at a crucial moment!

Stanley Simmons, who designed most of the lovely and effective costumes for our many musical productions at City Center, says that the main thing costume designers should keep in mind is that color and silhouette furnish the atmosphere and mood of a scene. Details are less important. This is particularly true in costuming for community theatre.

Every good costume designer knows that colors create mood. In this production of *Angel Street*, the victim wore white while the menacing husband dressed in stiff clothes with dark colors. *(Picture courtesy of the Sutter Buttes Regional Theatre, Yuba City, Calif.)*

chapter 9

Taking the Bows

THERE IS GLAMOUR in an opening night, any opening night. There is glamour and excitement, pleasure and expectation. Also, there are tension, tears, and unabashed fright. On Broadway, not only public and critical acceptance or rejection that will make or break a career is imminent, but a fortune in dollars is at stake. Hundreds of thousands ride on a dramatic play, and millions on the average new musical—a million to be speedily lost if all goes awry; many millions to be made if all goes well.

(Right here, I'd like to make a personal comment: when a show closes rapidly and the entire investment is "lost," it is not "money down the drain," as the media like to put it, as though the dollar bills had been poured into the sewer. The money is tax deductible for the investors and has been paid out to theatre people who have been working on the project sometimes for as long as six months or a year. It has not been a successful gamble for the backers, but it has kept a lot of artists and artisans working and able to continue in show biz.

In the community theatre it is not a livelihood or a large investment that are at stake, but a question of local pride, prestige, ego, and perhaps the ongoing progress of the theatre group. But whether on or off Broadway, or in a barn in Kansas, backstage on opening night is pretty sure to be a scene of tension, excitement and hopefully controlled emotion. Everyone who has had, or will have, anything at all to do with what will transpire when the curtain rises, or the lights go up on the playing area, is making last minute checks—actual or mental—to try to make sure that all will go smoothly and as planned.

When we think of opening night nerves, we usually mean the actors. They, however, are almost always the least apprehensive. If they have been properly rehearsed, are sure of knowing their lines, and are comfortable in their costumes and makeup, they are ready and even eager to get out in front of an audience and put into practice what they have been working on for so long. (My husband, who was a combat general in two wars, once said, "When men are properly trained, even for deadly warfare, they actually become impatient to go into action. They are ready to put into practice what they have learned.") Self-confidence is the key.

I recall the story of Ethel Merman on the opening night of *Annie Get Your Gun*. Joshua Logan, who had directed the musical, went into her dressing-room a few minutes before curtain time to wish her well and to give her final words of encouragement and assurance. He found her costumed and ready, lying back on her chaise-longue, calmly filing her nails.

"You're the most relaxed person in the theatre tonight," Logan exclaimed.

"Why not?" she asked. "I know my stuff. If the folks in the audience could do it, they'd be where I am instead of out front."

In the community theatre, if there is unease among the actors on opening night, the director may have been lax, or the actors themselves may have shirked their responsibilities to him and to the play. But also it could be due to some sudden change—some last minute replacement for an actor who has been taken ill, or had an accident, or some backstage worker who unexpectedly left the ranks. It might be an actor in a very unimportant part, or a third assistant stage manager, but the fact that there has been a break in the usual pattern is enough to upset the confidence that has been building up through weeks of work. When this is the case, it is the director's business to take a leaf from the book of a sports coach, and "pep talk" his players and backstage workers into a return of their self-assurance. All of them—actors, stage managers, stage hands, sound men, wardrobe people, light men—are listening for "half hour," "fifteen minutes," "five minutes," "places on stage, please" and "lights!"—like the count-down for the launching of a space satelite, and just as tension-building! Only the director, upon whom they all have been leaning, can offer them some sort of relief.

Not all directors, however, are willing to do this. Jed Harris, who directed so many of his own successful productions, would have a final run-through the afternoon before the opening, and at its conclusion he would assure the cast and the backstage workers that he had done all he could for them, and that he would not be at the theatre that night! "I don't believe in directors running backstage between the acts," he said. "There is a rhythm to a well directed play which even includes the intervals. No one, not even the director, should be allowed to interfere with that rhythm."

On the other hand, Jose Ferrer often acted in the plays he directed and he followed quite the opposite tactic, since he was right there on the scene. If all was going well—and it usually was—he would joke with his fellow workers between acts, or invite them into his dressing-room to chat about how the play was going. His relaxed and genial behavior loosened many a taut nerve.

Almost nothing could be worse for the morale of a company than a distraught director who makes no effort to hide his own lack of confidence in them and the play during the final dress rehearsals or run-throughs and on opening night. If things have been going wrong, it is better, as we said before, to postpone the opening and set them right. If all apparently has gone well, but the director still has doubts about some of his casting, or his choice of technicians, or even the way he has directed the play, he should face the fact that it is too late to do anything about it. It is up to him to hope for the best and put on a good face. Besides, miracles do happen in the theatre and openings always seem to turn out better than expected! Something about that sudden release of pent-up tension seems to result in everyone being just a little bit better than even he himself dreamed he'd be!

There are times, unfortunately, when the miracle doesn't happen, times when everything goes wrong, even after good dress rehearsals and previews. Cues are missed, actors forget their lines, lights go up at the wrong time or don't come on at all, an important prop is forgotten, other seeming calamities occur. Well, it has happened before and it will happen again, but life goes on and so does show business.

If the world has seemed to fall apart in the first act, perhaps things can be done to put it together again before the second act, even if the curtain must be down a little longer than usual. Hands can be held, tears can be dried, reassuring words and kisses can be given. Never, never must anyone rush backstage in a fit of furious fault-finding! No matter how devastated the director may feel at the shambles that has been made of his work of art, he must control his true emotions and just do his best to mend or put together what pieces are left. The more calm he can spread, the better the next act and the rest of the play will be.

But triumph or disaster, the play will come to an end—all too soon in the first case, none too soon in the latter. And then will come the taking of the bows, brief ones when the audience is disappointed or embarrassed, lengthy and involved ones when the audience is enthusiastically pleased. Applause must always be allowed to run its own course, neither stopped too soon nor milked for more. It is the audience's only way to not just show appreciation for what they have witnessed, but also the only way they can participate in what has been done.

Participation is very important to success in show business. Ballet succeeds because when Nureyev or Baryshnikov makes those thrilling leaps and turns with grace and beauty, everyone out front has done them with them. Likewise, when a play has been particularly enjoyable, all the best lines have been read by the audience. Their response, tangible to the actors, is absolutely necessary to the interaction which underlies every successful performance. In a sense they are applauding their own accomplishment. The Russians understand this and return the applause from the stage. (It seems charming when done by them, but when attempted by American companies, audiences sometimes seem less enchanted, even embarrassed.)

Curtain calls—or "taking the bows"—are part of the show and always should be rehearsed. They, too, must have a definite form and rhythm. The bows at the end of a comedy or musical can bring into play all of the director's ingenuity and whimsy. He can improvise additional bits of business that carry the action through the curtain calls with the actors staying in character. This is all to the good if not carried so far as to seem strained, or cutesy.

Traditional curtain calls usually start with the player of the least important role coming on stage, acknowledging the applause he receives with a quick but gracious bow, and taking a set place on stage. He is closely followed by the second least important character, and so on until the leading players have been applauded and the entire company is on stage. Then, joining hands—usually held out to the cast by the leading players—the company takes a well-timed and coordinated bow all together. If the applause continues, another company bow is taken. Then the curtain drops (or the lights go down if the company is in an open playing area), the lesser players leave the stage, and the curtain rises or the lights go up on the leading players alone. This is their special tribute. If after several bows the applause continues, the leading players bring back the entire company and they all continue concerted bows until the curtain falls for the last time.

This "last time" is usually judged by the stage manager, and it is important that he chose just the right psychological moment for it, neither too soon nor too late.

"Taking a bow," by the way, is the actor's acknowledgment of the public's approval and always must be executed graciously, as befits the acknowledgment of a compliment. There is something emotionally stirring in a well-taken bow. I have found myself with a lump in my throat when I have seen a great diva, or ballerina, or theatre star sink into a deep curtsy, head bowed low, as a gesture of appreciation for a great ovation.

Well, the curtain has fallen, the bows have been taken and the audience is filing out. If there has been music in the play, it is nice to keep it playing until the last patron has left. If there are no programs left behind it has been a gala evening indeed, and one to be long remembered.

Such evenings are what it is all about, what all of us work for and pray for. If it happens once in a lifetime, it should be enough. But fortunately one time whets the appetite for more. And so we work on, all the hundreds and thousands of us, in theatres great and small, in cellars, palaces, churches, arenas, lofts and barns.

May our trials and tribulations be lessened, and our triumphs be increased. But in any case, let us never lose hope nor do less than our best.

GLOSSARY of Theatre Terms

ACT CALL The stage manager's call to the actors to come on stage for the beginning of an act or a scene.

ACT CURTAIN The curtain which goes up at the beginning of each act or scene, or goes down to close the act or scene; usually the permanent theatre curtain, but sometimes specially designed curtains.

ACT WARNING The stage manager's warning of the amount of time to the beginning of an act or scene. Before the start of a play or show, the stage manager calls "half-hour," then "fifteen minutes," and "five minutes."

APRON The front part of the stage.

ASBESTOS The fire proof curtain mandatory in most professional theatres between the stage and the auditorium.

BACKING A drop or piece of scenery behind a window, door or other opening to mask the backstage area from the view of the audience.

BACK STAGE The stage itself; also the dressing-rooms, property room, storage space, everything back of the playing area.

BACK WALL The rear wall of a set, or the rear wall of the theatre itself.

BATTENS Strips of wood (usually 1" by 4" or 1" by 2") or pipes used at the top and bottom of scenery drops to make them hang smoothly.

BLACK OUT All stage lights out. Ends scenes and acts when no curtain is used, and for arena theatres.

BOOK The story and dialogue for a musical.

BOX OFFICE The place where the tickets are kept and sold.

CALL BOARD The bulletin board near the stage entrance on which the stage manager posts notices of rehearsal times and various other notices to the company. All actors and stage crew are instructed to look at the call board on entering or leaving the theatre.

CLEAR STAGE The stage manager's call just before the beginning of a scene or act asking all crew members to leave the stage.

CLOSE IN To bring together the two parts of a draw curtain, partially or entirely.

CURTAIN LINE The imaginary line where the front curtain on the stage floor when it is down. Also the line on which the front curtain is hung.

CYCLORAMA A curved canvas background surrounding the sides and the back of the acting area, painted usually to resemble the sky, or other distant vistas.

DOWN STAGE Toward the auditorium; toward the front of the stage.

DRESS PARADE A rehearsal when the actors wear costumes and make up for the first time to check on colors, fit, hair styles, etc.

DROP Any canvas painted as part of the scenery, hung from the grid, usually with battens at top and bottom.

FLAME PROOFING Fire-proofing by spraying with a ready prepared flame-proofing chemical liquid (obtainable from theatrical supply houses).

FLATS Pieces of scenery; a wooden frame covered by painted canvas.

FLIES The entire area above the stage, not visible to the audience, where scenery is hung.

FRONT OF THE HOUSE The lobby, box office, usually the manager's office and other offices. Also used to denote all activity and business not related directly to the production.

GELS (Gelatins) Colored sheets of thin plastic used in front of various stage lamps for color.

GRIPS Stage hands who handle the scenery.

GROUND CLOTH The canvas usually used to cover the stage or playing area floor.

GREEN ROOM The actors' lounge, where they receive visitors, etc. (Very useful, but unfortunately often non-existent.)

IN ONE The acting area at the very front of the stage.

LEFT STAGE or "Stage Left" is at the actors' left and at the right as viewed by the audience.

OFF STAGE Any part of the stage outside the acting area and not visible to the audience.

ON STAGE The stage manager's call to take places on stage.

OUT FRONT In front of the acting area; in the auditorium.

PRACTICAL Any piece of scenery or property used by the actors; A practical window or door is one which opens and closes.

PROMPT BOOK The copy of the play or show in which are noted all cues for lights, sounds, openings and closings of acts, descriptions of the actors' business and movements, etc. Used by the stage manager for running the show.

PROPERTIES (1) Scene props are all the things used to "dress" the stage setting: furniture, paintings, books, window curtains, rugs, etc. (2) Hand props are anything handled by the actors: cigarettes, pocketbooks, letters, food, dishes, matches, etc.

PROPERTY TABLE Table or tables placed off-stage near an entrance to the stage or playing area where hand props are laid out for the actors.

PROSCENIUM The architectural frame separating the stage from the auditorium.

PROPERTY MAN The person in charge of all props.

RAMP A sloping platform at an angle not too great for actors to walk on.

REVOLVING STAGE A large turntable in the center of the stage on which two or more sets can be placed and shown to the audience by swiveling the turntable.

RIGHT STAGE Or "Stage Right" is at the actors' right as they face the audience and at the left as viewed by the audience.

RING DOWN The signal for dropping the curtain or closing in the curtains at the end of a performance.

SETTING UP Placing the set on the stage, dressing it with the proper properties, mounting and focusing the lights, etc. Any one or all of these processes.

SCRIPT The written material for the play or show.

SCRIM A gauze curtain for a front drop used in transformation scenes; i.e., a scene is painted on the scrim which appears opaque, but when the front lights are taken off the scrim and the lights behind it are brought up, the scrim becomes semi-transparent and the setting behind it is seen.

SOUND EFFECTS The sounds of creaking doors, howling winds, thunder, approaching automobiles, distant train whistles, fog horns, etc., produced backstage, or from the wings.

STAGE BRACE A wooden brace of adjustable length with a hook at one end for fastening to an eye or cleat on the back of a flat of scenery and a foot iron at the other end, for screwing to the stage floor to brace a piece of scenery. (A foot iron is a steel brace bolted to the bottom of a piece of scenery so that it may be fastened to the stage floor by means of a stage screw.)

STAGE SCREW A steel screw with a handle for use with stage braces secure to scenery.

STAND BY The stage manager's call to be ready.

STAND-BY Some player paid to be ready to take on the role played by a member of a cast who becomes ill or is otherwise unable to play. Unlike an understudy, a stand-by is not obliged to report to the theatre at performance time, but must be within reach by telephone or messenger at all times.

STAGE MANAGER The person in charge of the production backstage, who sees that the play or show is performed as directed throughout the run. He is in charge of the prompt book and gives all cues for curtain, lights, sound effects, etc. Runs the show and is the backstage boss.

STRIKE The order given by the stage manager to the crew to clear the stage of the set and properties.

SIGHT LINES The lines of vision from various parts of the theatre or auditorium.

TECHNICAL REHEARSAL Held for the stage crew to become accustomed to handling the scenery, properties, etc., and for light cues to be followed, also sound effects, etc. Usually held in conjunction with the dress parade and with the cast to give the necessary cues. "Cue to cue" means for the actors not to play the entire scene, but to cut to the various cues necessary to the crew.

TIME SHEET Used by the stage manager to keep track of the time or hours worked by the stage crew, usually, in professional theatre, to avoid overtime charges.

TRAVELER A draw curtain which "travels" from left to right, or vice versa, at the front of the stage, or wherever needed.

UP STAGE Away from the footlights, if any, or front of the stage. Toward the back of the stage. Also to "up stage" an actor so that when speaking to him his back is almost to the audience.

WING A flat, or piece of scenery parallel to the front of the stage. "In the wings" means at the sides of the stage, unseen by the audience.